BEVERLEY DOUGLAS was born to 1964. She grew up in a loving home wi few recreation facilities at that time, cl in the street. Concerned parents lobbie play space was provided for all children. The disused colliery and stone yard around the corner from her house was transformed.

In 1972, Felix Road Adventure Playground was opened and Beverley has fond childhood memories of the times she spent enjoying the freedom of this special place.

At a young age, Beverley experienced racism and had to flee for her safety whilst walking home from a youth club. She also encountered many challenges within the education system, but that didn't stop her becoming a police officer.

In 1983 she joined the Avon and Somerset Special Constabulary. Five years later she joined the Regulars. After more than three decades of an enjoyable, sometimes challenging career, she retired in 2017.

Now she and her husband Richard live between the UK and Gozo, Malta where she continues to write.

Cutie.

BEVERLEY DOUGLAS

To

Elaine

Enjoy reading about my childhood.

Best wishes

Beverley Douglas

SilverWood

Published in 2021 by SilverWood Books

SilverWood Books Ltd
14 Small Street, Bristol, BS1 1DE, United Kingdom
www.silverwoodbooks.co.uk

ISBN 978-1-80042-106-6 (paperback)
ISBN 978-1-80042-107-3 (ebook)

British Library Cataloguing in Publication Data
A CIP catalogue record for this book is
available from the British Library

Page design and typesetting by SilverWood Books

Thank you, Mum and Dad, for bringing me into the world and for making me part of your lives. You made many sacrifices, taught me the difference between right and wrong, and how to forgive and be non-judgmental of others.

Now it is my turn to shape your history into my own interpretation of life's events. Like you, I hope to influence those around me in a small way, to help change the world and make it a better place for your grandchildren. I will continue to show them love and share all my happy memories of you.

I am so proud of all your achievements and will pass on your fascinating stories, which I will cherish forever.

Prologue

Dearest Mother And Father

Mum

My mother, Agatha Jean Douglas, née Moulton, was born in Kingston, Jamaica, on 31 May 1931. Her dad, Gilbert Moulton, who was born in 1907, owned a general store until he died at the age of sixty-seven in 1974. Her mum, Anita Picard, was born in 1905 and died in 1943 at the age of thirty-eight from consumption. Mum had an older brother, Arthur, born just one year before her, although there has always been some discrepancy about their actual birth dates. In Jamaica, if the children were not registered within a certain period, their parents would be fined. To avoid the payment, parents would lie about the date their child was born. However, in most cases this may have only been a couple of months. Mum's brother Arthur lived to a greater age than Mum, dying in 2005 at the age of seventy-five. They lived in Jamaica until their early twenties when, in 1953, Arthur emigrated to England, aged twenty-three. Mum followed him two years later and they both settled in Derby.

They were privately educated at a Catholic school in Kingston.

Their mum died unexpectedly when Arthur was fourteen years old and Mum was thirteen. She said that their mum's death came as a total shock to everyone. It was devastating and her brother changed overnight. They had always been close and he had looked out for my mum, but after their loss they drifted apart. Mum often heard her brother sobbing at night when everyone had gone to bed. She was too young to know how to console him and said that he became withdrawn and spent many hours alone.

He started rebelling at school, playing truant and, when he was there, starting fights in the playground, eventually falling behind with his studies. He mixed with the wrong crowd, staying out late, and got into trouble with the local police. His dad took him under his wing and set him to work in the family business where he would learn a good trade.

Mum finished her education, leaving school at the age of fifteen. Her desire was to continue studying at secretarial college, but her dad had other ideas for her future. Mum said that he bought her a sewing machine, which made her happy. When she was not working in the family store or managing the house, she made her own clothes to the envy of many. Her life was simple, having lost contact with her school friends who either lived too far away in the countryside or had returned to live abroad. Mum's only outlet was church on Sundays or Bible class one evening a week. She never mentioned any other family being around her as she grew up.

Neither her dad nor her brother had noticed that she was maturing into a young woman. She had a few admirers but, without female influence or guidance in her life, she made her own decisions when it came to relationships. She met a young man at church and courted him in secret. When she was not working in the store, she retreated to the confines of her bedroom, apparently reading or sewing. In fact, after dark she would climb out of her bedroom window and meet up with her young man. She continued her secret rendezvous throughout her teenage years.

8

Mum said that, initially, Arthur was happy working in the store and liked earning his own money. He was a good salesman, quick to learn about the business, and he loved dealing with the customers. On Saturdays, the store was always busy with eligible young ladies who came in with their mothers or chaperones to buy material, lace or ribbons. He enjoyed flirting with them and playing one off against the other with his charm. The ladies would be swooning after him as he moved around the store fetching their orders. Long after he had served them, they would continue to loiter, hoping that he might ask one for a date. If any lady caught his eye, he happily flirted with them, volunteering to deliver groceries to their homes. Under the watchful eye of their fathers, he boasted of the countless times he had spent alone with many pretty ladies, sitting on the porch with them after dark, drinking homemade lemonade or sipping ginger beer.

Away from the glare of his dad, Arthur began to tire of working in the store. He was working long hours and felt that he was missing out on the fun his friends were having. Mum said these friends started hanging around the store or distracting him away from his deliveries, leaving her to pick up the slack. He couldn't resist the temptation and soon slipped back into his old ways. He began drinking heavily, arriving home drunk, which always ended in heated arguments with their dad. He got into fights with anyone who crossed his path. The local police had also warned him of his unruly behaviour and lack of respect towards authority, but he continued to rebel. Their dad worried that it was only a matter of time before he got himself into serious trouble.

At his wits' end, Mum's dad confided in the preacher and his wife, who were close friends of the family. They convinced him that his children needed stability in their lives in the shape of a new mother. They introduced him to potential ladies who were keen to be married. He accepted many invitations to dinner or a stroll out with respectable single or widowed ladies who were connected to the church. A good-looking man of means and property, he was an exceptionally good catch for any woman. Mum remembers her dad dressed in his best suit and starched shirt, complete with trilby hat, looking very smart as he left home to pay the ladies a visit. She said that he enjoyed courting as the ladies were a welcome distraction from the store and her unruly brother. Once her dad had left the house for the evening, she and her brother would be left to refill the shelves in the store. Soon Arthur's friends would call upon him. Unable to resist the temptation, he would never miss the chance to make mischief in the village.

Eventually, their dad announced he was going to be married. Having met so many pleasant ladies, Mum said she was surprised at his choice. With her feet firmly under the table, their stepmum's only interest was in keeping an eye on the books and the weekly takings, which she would lock away in the safe. She stopped Mum from having the most lavish of materials or haberdashery, keeping the best for herself. Now a woman of means, her stepmum bought the best of everything. Even her undergarments were expensively made by the local seamstress. Mum said that she was strict and loved to criticise or scold her. Nothing Mum did was ever good enough. The stepmum took great pleasure in displaying her authority in front of her friends, whom she would invite around for afternoon tea. She berated their dad for the way he disciplined his children. Her dad got to the point where he seldom challenged his wife. Mum said that he never beat them, which made her stepmum angry. She also berated Arthur at every opportunity about his wayward lifestyle, as well as the bad company he kept. This would cause more arguments and drive him out of the house. Sometimes he disappeared for weeks, which was distressing for their stepmum and dad.

Arthur

Now in his early twenties, Arthur was still heavily involved with gangs and breaking the law. He seldom returned to the house as this caused arguments with his stepmum. There was always someone undesirable looking for him, which caused concern for everyone. Mum would meet her brother in secret away from the house, reporting back on any comings or goings. She also gave him money, food or clean clothes to tide him over.

Things came to a head when Arthur got into a fight and injured a well-connected man. The police came to the house to arrest him, but he had disappeared. He eventually turned up at the house weeks later to ask his dad for help. His dad was furious that he had brought trouble to his door, but didn't want his son to go to prison. He told him that the only way he would help him was if he agreed to leave Jamaica for a new life in England, so Arthur agreed. Being a well-respected, wealthy businessman, his dad was able to persuade the police not to pursue the investigation. The victim was also happy with the arrangement and was compensated for his inconvenience, and the matter was closed.

In 1953, aged twenty-three, Arthur boarded a flight from Jamaica to Heathrow, leaving Mum behind. They were very distraught at leaving each other, but vowed they would be together again one day.

Arthur stayed in London, then Chesterfield for a short time, before moving to Derby, where there was a large Jamaican community. Finding suitable accommodation was difficult due to prejudice. Many houses displayed signs in their windows saying "No Blacks, No Irish, No Dogs" – or, worse, he was told that the room had been taken. Few white people at the time would rent a room to people of colour, but eventually he found lodgings at an extortionate price with a widowed white woman. The house was overcrowded, damp, full of infestation and had no heating. For electricity, he had to put a shilling in the meter. Arthur said anyone who shared a room slept in shifts. As one person got up for work, the other was arriving home from a night shift and would jump into the still warm, empty bed. Everyone in the house would share the same bathroom and kitchen. As long as they all paid their rent on time, the landlady was happy. Living conditions were appalling, nothing like he had ever experienced in Jamaica, but he couldn't afford to go back home. A rude awakening, but at least he had a roof over his head.

While in Derby, Arthur met and married his wife, Jane. They had seven children together. He had several jobs including working on the buses, as well as on the railway for many years. He saved most of his money and then, after a year, was able to buy his first house. He rented out all the rooms to his friends, which gave him an extra income. Once they had established themselves, his friends also bought their own homes. He continued to receive new friends from Jamaica and this was one of the many ways Jamaicans were able to build strong communities together.

Years later he found a job at Rolls-Royce, where he worked until he retired. Not wishing to hang up his boots quite yet, he was then employed by Derbyshire Police as the school crossing lollipop man, a job he was extremely proud of.

Mum's adult years

Mum fell pregnant at the age of twenty, giving birth to Joseph in 1951. Three years later, she fell pregnant again with her daughter Merlene. She never talked about their dad. Then, when she was twenty-five, her dad sent her to England without the children. She never spoke of how she coped with leaving two small children behind in Jamaica or how it affected her as a young mum. Maybe her parents wanted her to have a better life, which they believed she could only achieve by moving abroad. Her brother Arthur was already in the UK, so at least she wouldn't be alone. Joseph and Merlene, my elder siblings, remained in Jamaica and were brought up by their granddad and Mum's stepmum until he died.

I never met my maternal or paternal grandparents, who all lived and died in Jamaica when I was young. Neither of my parents talked much about their own childhood, so over the years it has been difficult to piece together a clear story of their lives. This is common in Jamaican families of that generation. It was also common in large families for parents to leave their young children with grandparents while they travelled to England during the Windrush years.

In 1948, after the Second World War, the troopship *Empire Windrush* was the first vessel to bring West Indian immigrants from Jamaica to London, docking in the Port of Tilbury. With a labour shortage in state-run services within the NHS, London Transport and construction, many Caribbeans found work in post-war UK. Some stayed for a few years before returning to Jamaica while others remained, establishing new lives in Britain.

Once they had settled, they sent for their children to join them in the UK. I knew from a young age that I had an older brother and sister who lived in Jamaica, but I never knew until I was in my teens that we had different fathers. My dad treated them like the rest of his children, sending them regular letters, pictures or parcels so they were never excluded. Mum sent for them to join the family in the UK, but with her having three other children and mental health problems the authorities wouldn't allow them to come. This came as a shock to the family, but there was nothing anyone could do.

My parents returned to Jamaica in 1972 and Mum again in 1982. This was a significant time for her as she was able to rekindle her relationship with her children. My brother Joseph is married with four children. He now lives in America with his wife and the two younger children. His two older girls, who I've met, both live in Jamaica. My other siblings have all met Joseph, but because of circumstances we have never met.

I am in regular contact with my sister Merlene. We have a strong connection and a lovely relationship, having met for the first time in 1987 after Mum died. She lived in the UK for many years before returning to Jamaica and whenever I visit Jamaica, I spend time with her. I also spent years visiting my dad's sisters in Jamaica, who have since died.

Dad

My dad, Vincent Nathaniel Douglas, was born on 29 November 1929 in Point Hill, St Catherine, Jamaica. He was the youngest of six children born to Thomas Douglas, a cultivator who died in 1943. His mother, Ellen Douglas, née Davis, was born in 1903. She died of diabetes in 1969.

Dad went to the village school in Point Hill. When not at school, he spent much of his childhood helping his dad farm their five acres of land. He told stories of riding his donkey bareback through the bush, carrying water and food cooked by his mother to feed all the workers in the fields. He said that there was always singing, which could be heard across the valleys, as the workers tended to the sugar cane crops. They also planted ackee trees, yams and plantain, which would be harvested and sold at the market in Spanish Town. Coconut, banana and mango trees were abundant in Jamaica, as well as being an important part of the staple diet. His dad shared his crops with the workers and people in the village so everyone could feed their families. It also meant that no one went hungry or needed to steal food as there was enough for everyone. Other farmers in the village did the same. Dad often said almost every tree in Jamaica bears a fruit that can be eaten.

In his early twenties, while still living in Jamaica, Dad fathered his first child, Lilith, with his childhood sweetheart. They were not married. She was sent to England, leaving Lilith with her grandparents. He spent time looking after his daughter in the early years, with the help of his mother, until he too came to England in 1954. He had planned to be reunited with Lilith's mother, who was living in a shared house in London. However, when he arrived to be with her, she had other ideas about their relationship. She had met someone else. Dad never said how he felt, but it must have come as a big disappointment and shattered his dreams. I am not sure how long he remained in London, but his next stop was Derby where he knew friends from Jamaica.

Lilith came to England to join her mother, but I am not sure at what age. We all knew about her, though Dad never talked about her. When she was sixteen, she moved to America and lived with Dad's sister, Sephlyn. Lilith visited the UK when I was about seventeen and we met in Bristol for the first time. By then, I was not interested in what had happened in the earlier years, but I know Dad was pleased to see her and they remained in touch until Dad died. She was a lovely person, but we never developed a relationship, although I did try to contact her in later years. She has not been so forthcoming, but the door is always open.

My Parents' Meeting

Mum arrived in England in 1956 and, like Arthur, lived in London for a short time. However, she didn't stay there for long, moving to Derby to be with her brother. It was here that she met my dad, who was visiting friends in the same house she lived in, and their relationship blossomed. They soon moved in together and my sister Patsy was born in 1958, and my brother Keith a year later. That same year, Mum and Dad were married.

I don't know what Dad did for a job in Derby or where they lived, but what I do know is he said he needed a more stable job. He was interested in the construction industry, which was booming in the South West, so he moved the family to Bristol. To begin with, he found work in the building trade and they moved into a house in Camberley Road, Knowle. This is where my other sisters, Elaine, Yvonne and Veronica, were born in 1960, '61, and '62.

At that time there were few black or Asian families living in Knowle. The residents were predominantly white and working class, and indeed still are. With a young family, my parents were isolated and had no family support or friends from within their own community, which made life extremely difficult.

Patsy remembers that the family were regularly racially abused by the neighbours or random people in the street. More than once, Mum was spat at and reduced to tears. Patsy described a time when she and Keith saw someone posting faeces through their letterbox, and this happened on more than one occasion. It was heartbreaking for me to hear this when she said that they didn't understand why. She said that, by the time Elaine was born, Mum was suffering from ill health and had suffered a nervous breakdown. Dad did his best to support the family, but often the abuse happened while he was at work or when they were at school. Patsy talked of being severely bullied in the playground or racially taunted on her way to and from school – not only by kids, but by their parents, too. In the classroom teachers also ignored racist abuse, so sadly at a young age Patsy, Keith and Elaine experienced intolerable racism.

When Mum was admitted to hospital, Dad would take time off work to look after the family until she recovered. Patsy said people were less likely to abuse them when he was around as he was quick to verbally retaliate. The police did nothing to prevent this abuse of my family and when Dad complained to them, they simply told him, "If you don't like it, you don't have to stay here."

Dad told a story of when he and his friends walked into a pub in Bristol and the landlord said, "We don't serve monkeys in here." Although they were very angry and deeply offended, Dad didn't retaliate as they were outnumbered by all the white men who had surrounded them, so they left without making a fuss. Once outside they were chased down the street, so this was one of many occasions when they had to keep their wits about them. They reported the abuse to the police, but very soon realised they weren't on the side of the black man.

Dad said he never went to dances at The Glen in Clifton on a Saturday night unless he was part of a group. If they weren't attacked in the club by Teddy boys, there would always be a fight afterwards and they would be chased through the streets. It did not stop them going out, but they went out in groups and never took their wives or girlfriends with them. When I asked Dad why he put up with this behaviour, he said it was a matter of survival. The Jamaicans had made England their home and there was no way he was going to allow these people to dictate his life through racism or violence. He said, "Black people have to stand up for their rights." To the credit of the Windrush generation, they continued to challenge racism and fight inequality for the benefit of us all. I am very proud of all their achievements.

Dad worked on the Severn crossing prior to its opening in 1966. I remember him telling me that he and a group of other workers nearly lost their lives while being ferried in a small boat across the estuary to carry out work on the footings of the bridge. It was a cold, blustery morning. All the men were nervous and reluctant to make the crossing because of the unpredictable gales, high winds and crashing waves threatening their safety. As the boat sailed into the wind, it began to take on water and the engine stalled. Dad said the skipper tried in vain to restart it without success and everybody began to panic. Without warning, a large wave upended the boat, tossing it into the air before it crashed down in the middle of the channel, throwing everyone into the freezing, ice-cold, treacherous, rough sea. With no one to rescue them, the men watched on in horror, treading water. The skipper desperately fought against the waves and swam towards the upturned vessel. He managed to right the rocking boat and clambered in. After several attempts he started the engine. Slowly, the boat circled the men, now frozen to the bone and disorientated, then one by one they were pulled back into the unsteady boat. Clinging onto the sides, they were all taken safely back to the shore. Once on the slipway and realising that they had reached dry land, the men embraced each other and thanked God that they had made it.

Dad said that he had never been so scared in his life. He was the happiest man alive when he realised that all the men had survived this terrible ordeal. He said it was sheer willpower and determination on the part of the skipper that kept the men afloat and saved them all. After that accident, he said everyone refused to work on the foundations in such poor conditions.

Dad also said it was depressing during the winter months having to work long hours outside. He was constantly exposed to the harsh winter weather, often working in the pouring rain or in sub-zero temperatures out in the middle of nowhere. I remember him coming home after a long day, soaked to the skin and freezing cold. As he rubbed his frozen hands over the paraffin heater, he talked of the biting cold winds penetrating his body, so much so that not even a pair of well-insulated gloves or boots kept his fingers or toes from freezing. He took to wearing Mum's tights under his trousers and long johns while at work, just to keep himself warm.

In between contracts, Dad got a job working on the buses after the Bristol Bus Boycott of 1963. The Bristol Omnibus Company, which was run by the local council, refused to employ black or Asian people to work on the buses. No non-white driver or conductor had ever been employed on the network. When a black man applied for a job with the company, he was invited in for an interview. However, when they saw that he was black, he was told that all the jobs were filled. This was obviously not true. The Bristol West Indian Development Council was formed by local Jamaicans, who for several months protested about the 'colour bar' and injustices towards people of colour. With the support of many white people and national media coverage the ban was lifted, allowing black and Asian people to work on the buses.

Dad once described a time while working on the buses as a conductor. He was on the top deck, issuing tickets to the passengers, when a white man racially abused him. He ignored the abuse but tried to issue him with a ticket. The man told him to "go back to his own country". Dad said he was furious. Without thinking of the consequences, he dragged the man from his seat, summoned the bus driver to stop and threw him off. Everyone applauded Dad as he resumed his duties. Incidents of racial abuse were a common occurrence, so he decided to leave the bus company.

In the early 1970s, he returned to work in construction and was employed by Laing and McAlpine. He told me that he was one of a few black men who worked on construction sites in the '60s. Both the black and Irish men encountered racism, but without them the industry would have suffered from labour shortages. He said that the management recognised their skills and my dad was good at his job. He got into scuffles with the English workers, but he refused to be intimidated and generally managed to sort out any differences they had. He fought racism with intellect and determination for years, defending not only his colour but the right to live in the UK. Working conditions for black people were not ideal and Dad often considered walking off the job, but he needed to provide for his family and the construction industry paid better than other employers. Dad made it clear he wasn't going anywhere. I think in time the English workers realised that they needed one another to get the job done.

Dad was responsible for operating huge earth-moving equipment, which was used in the building of many of the motorways that people drive along today. Some of the wheels on these machines were even taller than him. He was the foreman on many jobs, which took him all over the South West and Wales. He worked with both English and Irish men and was also responsible for transporting them to different sites. Sometimes Dad would come home in his works van and we would wait in the front garden for him to arrive. I remember him pulling up outside our house in a coach with several of his workmates on board. As they got off, they called out, "See you tomorrow, Snowy." My siblings and I would jump on the coach while Dad took us on the short drive around the corner where he parked it up for the night, then we would race him back to the house. When I asked him why the men had called him Snowy, he said that most sites were poorly lit or pitch-black and it was difficult to find anyone. He always wore a suit with a white shirt under his overalls. The men said that he was easy to recognise because his shirt was so white. Whenever it snowed it would settle in his hair, which amused the men, and the name just stuck. Dad made many friends and was well respected.

He retired early after a heart attack and in his late forties he bought a green Ford pickup truck, becoming an odd-job man. The truck came in useful as he helped his friends on small building projects. He would collect or deliver building materials for extra cash and help people with removals, as well as house clearances. I was about fourteen when he suggested I could earn extra money by helping with his deliveries. It was hard work moving sand and cement or breeze blocks, which gave me blisters, but a good way to earn myself extra cash.

Dad liked a drink and spent much of his time socialising at the local pub, The Lebeq. It was just around the corner from our house on Stapleton Road. It was there that he and his workmates would often stop off for a pint after work before he came home for his dinner. He would watch the evening news and fall asleep in the chair, before going down to the pub again, leaving us at home with Mum. Mum was not a drinker, but Dad, on the other hand, was in The Lebeq every night. He was also a member of the darts team.

I remember Mum would send me with my siblings down to the pub when she fancied a bottle of shandy. Kids were not allowed in pubs then, so we would stand in the foyer behind the frosted window and ring the bell. The landlord would slide the door open and you could see into the crowded, smoke-filled bar. Invariably you would recognise a few faces. The landlord over time got to know who you had come to see and would summon Dad to the door. He would come out with a drink for Mum and peanuts, crisps and Coca-Cola before sending us on our way. Other nights he would bring home fish and chips from the Chinese chip shop across the road.

Dad was a huge cricket fan and would spend hours watching the game on the television. I remember thinking it was the most boring sport that man had ever invented. For me, it was like watching paint dry. His favourite team was Jamaica, but he was very fond of the English team, too. My only regret was that I never took him to a live match at the Bristol County Ground; he would have loved it.

I could not have been more than nine years old and living in Lansdown Road when I was old enough to understand that Mum was having a breakdown. I remember Dad calling the doctor and telling us that Mum was not very well. He would take her to hospital where Mum would stay for a time, though I don't remember how long she was absent for. I only understood that the hospital would make her better, then she would come back home. My siblings were old enough to look after me and, as we were all at school during the day, Dad was able to go to work. Everyone rallied around until he came home in the evenings and cooked dinner. Life seemed normal to me as I always had my family around to look after me.

I don't know how many times Mum had taken ill when I was a child, but I do remember visiting her while she was in Barrow Gurney psychiatric hospital. Mum was diagnosed with depression, but I believe her condition of postnatal depression was misdiagnosed and she became very dependent on antidepressants. Severe stress and anxiety, coupled with racial hatred, also added to her emotional state, affecting her health. If she was diagnosed today, I believe her condition may have been diagnosed very differently. She never seemed that bad to me, other than maybe a little quiet. Nevertheless, she was always warm and loving towards me.

When Mum was well enough to come back home, she seemed to settle back into home life fairly quickly. We would smother her with love, help with the daily chores and be on our best behaviour. She slept a lot, which was probably the result of the medication she was on.

I learnt when I was in my late teens that she remained on antidepressants for many years. I discovered that she kept them in her bedside drawer, which rattled whenever she opened it. One day I asked her what the tablets were for. She had no issue telling me that they were for her bad nerves.

I am sure the route of her ill health was due to leaving her young children, family and friends in Jamaica in the 1950s to live in the UK, where the streets were not paved with gold. Instead, they were saturated in a deep depression of gloomy dark days and nights, where icicles formed on the insides of the windows and the biting cold penetrated her body, even though she was fully clothed. Living among people who hated her because of the colour of her skin or being compared to a dog when looking for somewhere to live could only have added further insult to injury. Such indignities could only amount to the loneliness and severe depression she endured. Nevertheless, England was the country she grew to call home.

Mum was a housewife and when well enough she worked part-time at Purdown Hospital as a domestic cleaner. My parents loved reggae music and had a great collection of records. On Sundays, the house would be alive with all the latest hits that were produced by Trojan Records. Dad also had a collection of music by members of the Rat Pack, as well as country and western artists. Music was a big part of their heritage and identity. Without a doubt, certain records reminded them of happier times they had while growing up in Jamaica. Their legacy is very much the genetic identity of who I am, so over the years I have built my own collection of records and CDs, but I still have many of their old records, too.

Eventually, with six small children to bring up, my parents moved to St Paul's where there was a strong black community. They settled there until Dad purchased a house in Lansdown Road, Easton, where I grew up. This is where he remained until he died after a long illness on 25 December 1999.

Chapter 1

Cutie Makes An Entrance

I was born in Southmead Hospital, Bristol, on 28 July 1964, Tuesday's child. I'm told that when I was born my dad looked at me and said I resembled his niece, whom he spent a lot of time with as a young man, growing up in Jamaica. She was given the nickname Cutie, hence my family's nickname for me to this day was passed down. Apparently, I was a lovely baby, but no lovelier than my siblings, of which there are eight, with me being the youngest. Nine of us in all!

My earliest memories are of living in a terraced house in Martin Street, St Paul's, when I was about four years old. It was a long street with houses on either side, which has since been demolished to make way for flats. The street name was also changed. At the time, there were lots of other black and Asian families who also lived on our street.

I can't remember much about the inside layout of the house, but I do remember that whenever it rained the roof leaked. The water would pour down the sides of the wall, forming puddles on the kitchen floor. Mum had to put out buckets to catch the dripping water between the hallway and the back room, to stop it running towards the front door or into the front room. When the rain eased, the dripping would stop and Mum would mop up and empty the bucket out into the street. Dad tried his best to patch the leaky roof, but it was an old house so he never quite managed to stop it. With the next downpour the roof would leak in a different place, much to his annoyance.

As well as the house being damp, it was infested with mice, so every night before we went to bed, he placed traps in the back room and kitchen with pieces of bacon or bread to tempt them. Overnight they would take the bait, be trapped and remain in the snare until morning, to Dad's delight. This was common in these old houses and something we all got used to. We spent most of our time in the back room, which had a coal fire. It was probably the warmest room in the house, close to the kitchen and where Mum could keep an eye on us. The back garden was small, so my siblings were forced to play either in the street or on the bomb site close to the house.

Although not devout Christians, every Sunday we all attended a church service in the Gospel Hall on St Nicholas Road. It had a nice family atmosphere and everyone was made to feel welcome. Sadly, now the Gospel Hall has also been demolished to make way for new houses.

Mum said not all churches were this welcoming towards black families. Her friends spoke of the shock and hurt of being turned away by, say, the Anglican or Baptist church when they were told not to come back. This snub encouraged black people to have prayer meetings in their own homes and turn them into a church on Sundays. Across the country, black-led Evangelical churches sprang up and welcomed their own followers for worship, becoming an integral part of the black community.

After church we would spend many happy hours playing in St Agnes Park on Thomas Street before returning home. Mum met lots of black friends that she knew in the park. She would happily sit for hours chatting while we played with the other kids we knew from church or who lived on our street. Our special play area housed brightly coloured swings, two slides and a climbing frame, as well as a shiny upright water fountain. I can still see it in my mind's eye today, everything surrounded by plush mature trees, flowering shrubs and sweet-smelling hedges buzzing with insects.

Throughout the year, the leaves constantly changed colour, marking the seasons: blossom in the spring, vibrant green during the hot summer and golden orange and brown welcoming the autumn, making it an interesting place to be. My favourite trees were the sycamore and conker trees. I was fascinated by the way the sycamore shed its seeds, especially when the wind carried thousands of them into the air. Swirling frantically, rotating at different angles, eventually scattering onto the ground. The conker trees' seeds were plush and green-covered with spiky tentacles on the outside. When they were ripe, they would fall out of the tree, hitting the ground with a thud.

My brother Keith would gather the fallen conkers, stuff them into his coat pockets and take them home. I would watch as he carefully prised open the outer pod to reveal the shiny brown conker inside. He would place them on the window ledge for a few days until they were hard. With one of Mum's knitting needles, he would carefully pierce a hole right through the centre, then thread it with string. The conker would be ready for a prearranged conker match, which would take place with his friends in the park after church the following Sunday.

The gardens across the road from the park were equally established with mature trees and climbing shrubs. There was a beautiful weeping willow rooted in the centre of the garden, which fascinated me. I loved the way it danced lazily in the breeze and I remember weaving in and out of its swaying branches as I played chase with my sisters. Collapsing, exhausted, on the well-kept grass, we would busy ourselves looking for four-leaf clovers or making daisy chains. I'm afraid I wasn't particularly good at making them, but I was happy to wait patiently until my sisters made a pretty necklace for me.

Among the flowering shrubs were several varieties of colourful roses, which were highly scented and gave off a lovely smell. I often chose a spot, not too far away from my sisters, to sit quietly enjoying the different fragrances around me. I was fascinated by the bumblebees hovering above the open rose petals. Slowly they would disappear inside for a few moments, then reappear before moving onto the next one, unaware that I had been watching them.

My sister Patsy said that Martin Street was a happy place for the family because they were surrounded by people like us, people of colour, so we never suffered racism. We all attended Newfoundland Road School, which was very multicultural. She said it was not without its issues and our parents went to the school on more than one occasion to deal with the staff. They made sure that we were protected and no one took advantage of the Douglas family. From a young age, I remember my parents telling us to be proud of where we came from. To never stay silent, but to challenge unfairness and inequality. Avoid a fight, but if need be, we should defend ourselves and always look after each other. As I grew much older, I remained positive, knowing that I was protected by my parents and supported by numerous community activists who tirelessly fought for equality.

Also in Martin Street was a corner shop owned by two sisters, Gladys and Eva Cook. We often went there to buy sweets. Patsy, who would have been ten years old, remembers keeping some of her collection money from Sunday school to buy sweets from the shop. She said Mum never knew that she kept the money, otherwise there would have been trouble. When I went into the shop, I remember reaching over the counter with two old pennies, which would buy me a bag of Black Jacks and Fruit Salads. The sisters were always nice to us. If ever I went into the shop with Mum, Mrs Cook would always give me a couple of gobstoppers while they gossiped for ages. I never complained, though, as I happily chomped on my sweets.

I am pleased to say that the play area still exists and is now the site of St Paul's Adventure Playground. The gardens across the road continue to be a well-maintained community garden.

Chapter 2

The Cake Shop

My brother Keith took me to Newfoundland Road School for a short time before he went on to senior school. After that, I would walk to school with my sister Veronica until I was old enough to go on my own.

Keith would wheel his bicycle out of the house and rest it up against the wall as I looked on. After checking the tyres, he would climb astride his bike, then lift me onto the handlebars, wrapped in my gloves and woolly bobble hat pulled down over my ears, with my feet dangling to one side. He would glance behind him, making sure the traffic had cleared. He would then slowly push himself off from the kerb while I snuggled into his chest. Freewheeling down the road, the piercing wind would sting my cheeks as we wobbled along. Our first stop was always to the cake shop in Seymour Road, which was just a short journey from our house.

Some of our friends lived in the three-storey terraced houses on either side of the road. I often wondered what went on behind the closed doors of their houses. How did they feel pulling back the curtains as the daylight flooded into their rooms? Was it the same disappointment I often felt when gazing out onto another dreary, wet winter's day? Perhaps the kids squabbled to be the first to use the only bathroom in the house. Did they have the same choices for breakfast as I had: porridge, Rice Krispies, tea, toast or hot chocolate? Obviously, I would never know the answers to any of these questions, but it was always fun trying to guess.

We would also pass other kids walking to school, braving the cold, some with their parents or older siblings, but I preferred being carried on my brother's bicycle. The postman would be out early, delivering letters to every house, as well as the milkman, dropping off milk and collecting the empties before climbing onto his milk float. If it were quiet enough, you could hear the whirr of the electric motor propelling him along, accompanied by the clattering of empty bottles.

Eventually, we stopped outside a battered red door. Tovey's fish shop was a few doors away and it always smelt of rancid, stale fish. The footpath outside was covered in bits of rotten fish and ice at that time of day, so people had to tread carefully. Pinching my nostrils together to block out the smell helped slightly as Keith carefully lifted me off the handlebars and set me down onto the ground beside him. He got off, too, and leant his bike against the wall. The door was slightly ajar and I could smell the unforgettable aroma of fresh bread wafting through the door. Holding my hand, he pulled me through the open door and together we squeezed into the dark room inside the bakery. Easing ourselves around the bags of unopened flour, we carefully moved between the racks of freshly baked, cooling bread and headed to the front of the bakery. Three large men covered in flour, wearing white overalls and floppy hats, greeted us with smiling faces. The one with ginger hair spoke first.

"Hello, lad. Who's this you've brought with you?"

29

"Oh, she's my little sister. Have you got any cakes? She'd like a doughnut."

"Eh, lad. How many do you want?"

"Two for me and two for her, please."

The man pulled out a tray from the rack full of an assortment of delicious cakes, some with sugar coatings and others with icing sugar. I watched in disbelief as he carefully scooped the doughnuts into a bag. He replaced the tray and smiled at me as he handed Keith the bulging bag. Keith paid him sixpence and we promptly went on our way.

"See you tomorrow, lad," he shouted as we left the bakery.

Keith handed me the bag and I pulled out a doughnut and greedily bit into the sugary dough. A stream of sticky, red jam oozed out of the top and the sugary coating stuck to my lips.

"Nice?"

Chomping and licking my fingers, I smiled and nodded my head.

"Come on, otherwise we'll be late for school."

I trotted behind him as he wheeled his bicycle, and sucked on my fingers, not wishing to miss any bits of the jam that covered my tiny hands. As we neared the school boundary wall, I could see the children rushing towards the gates; the bell was sounding for the start of the school day. Still licking my lips, I quickened my pace to arrive just in time.

"See you at break time."

Without another word, my brother had gone.

If we were running late, there would be no time to eat our cakes on the way to school. Instead, Keith would balance me on top of his handlebars while I held onto them tightly. He was always careful as he negotiated with the heavy rush hour traffic, as cars, buses and large trucks raced by without giving him much space. His task was made more difficult as the large dumper trucks belched out thick, smelly grey exhaust fumes, filling the air as well as my tiny nostrils, choking my lungs and forcing me to cough. I had to cover my face with my hands to block out the smell. The last stretch of the journey was much more enjoyable when we turned off the main road into a side street, leaving all the vehicles to continue their journey.

I continued to visit the bakery even after decimal currency came in and the cakes doubled in price. They still tasted just as good. I introduced a few of my friends from the adventure playground to the cake shop and we spent our pocket money in there for many years after that first visit with my brother.

Chapter 3

Early School Days

My first memory of preschool was at the age of four when I attended St Agnes playgroup, which was part of St Agnes Church in Thomas Street, St Paul's. I remember crying on my first day and every other day when Mum tried to leave me, so she took to staying at the back of the hall until I had been distracted with a dolly or a pushchair. At the end of the session, she would collect me and we would go into the park, where I would continue to play with all the other children.

At the age of five, I started at Newfoundland Road Primary School. I can't remember any of the children from the playgroup joining me when I was placed in Mrs Price's class. She was an older woman with greying hair, which she wore in a short bob. Her eyelids were blue, which I realised was eyeshadow as I got older. She wore lots of silver bangles up her arms, which made loud jingling noises every time she moved. I hadn't been in the class long when I witnessed a small boy being beaten by her in front of everyone. He was standing in line with his writing book, waiting to be seen at her desk. She became angry, started shouting at him, thrust him across her lap, pulled down his short trousers and spanked him violently several times on his bare backside.

I stared back in horror as the poor boy screamed out in pain. Once she had finished, she pulled up his shorts and sent him to sit in the book corner. I have no idea what this poor boy had done to deserve such abuse, but I very quickly decided that it was never going to happen to me. When school was over, Veronica collected me from the classroom. We met up with Elaine and I told them what Mrs Price had done to that poor boy. I was adamant that I was never going back to school ever again. Elaine was furious.

As we approached the end of my road, I could see Mum leaning on the gate, looking out for us. We all raced up the road to be the first to greet her. I was only halfway up the road by the time Elaine had reached the gate. I arrived gasping to catch my breath. Mum immediately demanded to know what had happened at school. Before I could finish, she was cursing loud enough for the whole street to hear.

The following day Mum walked us to school. She ushered us into the head teacher Miss Abbott's office and started cursing again. Elaine remembers Mum telling her that under no circumstances should anyone put their hands on any of her kids, otherwise there would be hell to pay. As we walked down the corridor, Mum's voice could still be heard. She continued to tell Miss Abbott that she was fed up with being racially abused and wouldn't allow anyone to touch her kids, especially if they had done nothing wrong. Although nothing had happened to me, Mum was clearly not taking any chances. I later found out that a few other West Indian parents had also paid visits to Miss Abbott.

Mrs Price continued to lose the plot, but never with me. I also remember witnessing her slap another boy on the back of his legs. Thankfully, however, most of the children avoided such violent treatment and she did have a kind side to her when she wasn't dishing out corporal punishment.

I'm not saying that I didn't get into trouble at school. I was no angel. I believe any punishment that I received was always proportionate, but those incidents I witnessed in class left me emotionally scarred for many years.

I was quite boisterous, so I also played with the boys when they allowed me to. I remember getting into a fair bit of trouble when I hung around with them and being sent to the headmistress. I can't remember what for, but I would have to stand outside her office facing the wall and I was rarely alone. I also remember having to miss out on some playtimes and being sent to the hall, where I had to write lines as a punishment for being late.

In the '70s, every child was given a free bottle of milk at school. I remember being milk monitor, whose job it was to hand out milk to everyone in class. There were always spare ones left over, so Mrs Price would give them to us monitors. We would sit in the book corner and drink our milk while she read stories of our choosing to us, prior to going home at the end of the day. This was also a time when she would reward us with different coloured stars for the good work we did in class.

By the time I was seven years old, I had moved up into the next two classes. My teachers, Mr Everett and Mr Patterson, were very sporty. We played lots of games outdoors, which came naturally to me in that I was good at running fast, I could change direction with ease and I could climb the ropes. I also loved gymnastics as my coordination and balance were good.

Every week my class went to Broad Weir Swimming Baths, which is where I learned to swim. By the time I was eight, I had swum my first width of the pool. For this achievement, I was presented with a certificate during morning assembly by Miss Abbott on 6 December 1972. The following October she presented me with my second certificate for swimming a hundred yards of the pool.

It was by sheer chance that I recently stumbled across an envelope containing every school report that was ever written about me between 1972 and 1980. I also found every athletics and swimming award from 1977 through to 1979, as well as all the records of my involvement with St John Ambulance.

However, good as I was at games, I wasn't so successful with my reading or writing and continued to struggle with education throughout my life. I was never assessed or tested for dyslexia or any other educational special needs. Therefore, as with many other children, I just existed in a system that disappointingly failed me. By the time I had reached secondary education, my reading ability was still poor. I found it difficult to string two sentences together without stumbling over each word and none of the teachers seemed bothered about it. There were other kids in the class who also struggled with reading out loud, so I thought it was normal.

Newfoundland Road School was demolished to make way for a new road that eventually linked into the start of the M32. Everyone moved to Cabot School, which was built to replace my old school. It was very modern and had new furniture and up-to-date facilities. Some of the staff members had changed, but everything else remained the same.

In the final year of being at Cabot School, I remember arriving on the last day of term and the end of an era. It was 1974 and I was ten years old. There were emotional farewells from children and staff, but the impact of moving on didn't faze me. As everyone gathered into the big hall to learn of their fate, I felt excited. I hadn't considered that this would be the last time I would see my friends. I could only think of the joy I felt knowing there would be no more assemblies or singing hymns from the book of John Wesley.

Miss Abbott stood behind the rostrum and handed out certificates of achievement to a handful of kids. I was sure that I wouldn't be one of them as I was far from a star pupil and often late for school. She wished everyone good luck before she announced the different schools each of us would be attending.

We all stood waiting expectantly as one by one she called out our names and we were instructed to leave the hall for the last time. Standing next to my friend Gary, whom I had formed a bond with, we waited to hear our fate. Not only were we in the same class, but we also lived near each other in Easton and often walked to and from school together. As luck would have it, Miss Abbott announced that Gary and I were both going to St George School. We smiled at each other as we exited the hall, both relieved that at least we knew each other.

Most of the kids at my primary school lived in and around the school catchment area and would continue to attend schools close to their homes. Gary and I lived on the other side of town, so the closest school in our catchment area was St George. With older siblings already attending that school, it made sense that we would follow in their footsteps.

Gradually, during the day, the walls in my classroom for the last year were stripped bare. All the pictures and poems that had taken pride of place now found themselves in the rubbish bin, which was sad to see, knowing everyone had worked so hard to receive their gold stars. When no one was looking, I rescued my chocolate-box drawing of a paddle boat, which I had sailed in on one of the few occasions I visited Eastville Park. The water was green with moss and I'd painted a ripple effect on the water. I folded it neatly into four and placed it inside my pocket.

"Snap!" Gary plonked himself on the chair next to me and pulled out a picture from inside his trouser pocket. He unfolded it to reveal a colourful picture of a castle.

"This is the castle my dad took me and my brothers to in the school holidays. I think it was in Wales."

"It's lovely." It suddenly dawned on me that it was just the two of us going to the same school, but there was no guarantee we would be together in the same class.

"Do you think that we'll be alright at our new school?"

"Yeh, I can't see why not." His broad cheeky smile made me feel a little more reassured.

"I hope so."

The bell sounded for lunch and we scrambled out of the class towards the dining hall. The dinner ladies had laid on a special buffet of sandwiches, sausage rolls, crisps and fancy cakes. We were also given orange squash instead of water, which was a real treat. In the playground there was a real buzz and sense of pride when the staff referred to us all as the 'leavers'. Although excited, there was also a feeling of sadness as I was moving on and I didn't know if I would ever see my friends again.

The bell sounded for the end of the day. One by one, we filed out of the class. Mr Nutter, my teacher, and all the other members of staff followed us out into the playground to bid us our final farewell. Without looking back, Gary and I slowly walked our familiar route home together for the final time. With little to say, we reached the final juncture, each vowing to see the other in September.

It's uncanny that Gary and I followed each other through the education system and we remained in the same class until we left secondary education.

Chapter 4

Lansdown Road, Easton

In 1969, when I was five years old, my family moved to our new home in Lansdown Road, Easton. It was a large, bright and airy three-bedroom terraced house that always got the sun. Downstairs there were two living rooms, the kitchen and a scullery. The back room or living room was where the television was housed. It had an open fire, which was our only source of heating, but if the fire wasn't lit we would use the paraffin heater instead. Dad made some changes to the house, extending the scullery, turning it into the kitchen. The old kitchen became the living room and he turned the old living room into their bedroom, freeing up the upstairs bedrooms for me and my siblings. We had a small front garden, which had a footpath leading up to the front door and a narrow flower bed where Mum would plant her favourite flowers, daffodils and foxgloves. The rear garden was a lovely sun trap. It had a small turfed area where Dad planted vegetables and a tool shed for anything he collected and couldn't bear to part with. The rest of the garden was concreted after Dad extended the kitchen.

Our house was always a hive of activity and I have fond memories of playing with the many kids Mum looked after over the years during the school holidays, so their parents could continue to work. We spent many hours playing bat and ball, football or cricket together in the back garden. If the ball went next door, we always had a spare. If not, we would dare each other to climb over the wall to retrieve it, avoiding getting caught.

Every Caribbean household I visited as a child had a best or front room. It was strictly out of bounds for us kids, only to be used when we had friends, family or visitors who came to see my parents. Mum and Dad also used it every Sunday to play their record collection on the radiogram, stacking up to six records under its arm, which would drop down on the deck one by one, before having to reload it. As we got older, Mum would allow us to sit in the front room and listen to the records unsupervised. When I was in my teens, I was allowed to listen to the Top 40 on a Sunday night. Once I bought my own records, I was also able to play them when I wanted on the radiogram.

Spending time in the front room was a real treat. Mum had a large collection of ornaments displayed around the room, as well as a glass cabinet that housed all her best glassware. Nothing was ever out of place. There was a large ornate fireplace in the centre of the feature wall, which was never used, so eventually Dad replaced it with a gas fire. The brown and orange three-seater sofa was large enough to sit four people. It was comfortable compared with the one in the back room that we used daily. Shoes were not allowed to be worn inside the front room as Mum didn't want to ruin the carpet.

Like many Jamaican women, Mum had her own electric sewing machine and made most of our clothes. I used to watch her making garments. I tried to use it, but it was too fast so I stuck to threading the needle or refilling the bobbin instead.

Stapleton Road was the place where everyone did their shopping, a busy road awash with thriving small businesses who traded in everything from groceries to ironmongery. There was also a doctor's surgery and a dental practice. All this changed when the road was severely affected by the building of the A432, which completely bisected the road in the 1970s, causing a large gap. Many shops closed, forcing the steady decline of the corner shop as people began to shop in Broadmead, preferring the big supermarkets. However, there were two Asian shops that survived. Mr Suba Singh's International Store was at the end of my road, while around the corner on Stapleton Road was the other Mr Singh's shop. Both supplied everything that was needed to cook Caribbean food, which you couldn't buy anywhere else.

Whenever I went into Mr Suba Singh's shop, he would greet me with a smile and say in his strong Indian accent, "Hello, my beauty, what can I do for you?" I would hand him my list of groceries and as he fetched everything he would sing.

"Take me to Jamaica where the rum come from, the rum come from, the rum come from. Take me to Jamaica where the rum come from and I drink with my beauty."

He was so funny that everyone in the shop would laugh at him.

A typical Caribbean shopping list would consist of: saltfish or dried salted cod (the cod is preserved with salt and you have to soak it before cooking), Jamaican bread (hard-dough bread, which is more dense than other breads and tends to be sweeter), sugar cane (peeled and chewed to obtain the juice), Jamaican patty (a savoury and spicy pastry filled with meat), callaloo (a spinach-like vegetable), yams, green banana, plantain (like bananas boiled or fried), okra (ladies' fingers), sweet potatoes, Scotch bonnet peppers, avocado, mango, cornmeal, peas (in fact, kidney beans or gungo peas, which would go into a pot of rice to make rice and peas for Sunday dinner), bulla cake (rich flat cake) and spice bun or Easter cake (sweet loaf). These small shops continue to provide such groceries for the staple diet of the Caribbean and Asian communities.

Across the road from our house, there was a sweet shop owned by Mrs Denvour, who was well into her eighties but sharp as a button.

The shop was small and smelled musty, but she still did a good trade selling boiled sweets and cigarettes. Mum, who fondly referred to her as Mrs D, kept an eye on her, doing the odd errand while my sister Yvonne often did her shopping on a Saturday and would be rewarded with sixpence. I seldom went into her shop alone as Mum didn't like me crossing the busy road, which was used by the local buses going to and from the depot, as well as being a thoroughfare for all traffic before the dual carriageway was built. When Mum and Dad moved out of the front bedroom and I shared it with Yvonne, these buses often kept me awake as they rumbled up and down the road during the early hours of the morning.

When I was about ten, I got knocked over by a car while crossing the road after buying a bag of sweets from Mrs D's shop. I hadn't asked my mum if I could go to the shop because she would have said no. It was about 5pm. The road would have been busy, plus it had been raining heavily. There were cars parked outside our house, which made it difficult for me to see if the road was clear. However, I managed to cross safely and bought my sweets. I came out of the shop and, without looking, stepped off the kerb right into the path of an oncoming car. I heard the screech of tyres before the car hit me, knocking me over into the wet road. Feeling dazed and frightened, I sat there for a few moments before coming to my senses as the wet rain soaked through my clothes.

Like a scared rabbit in the headlights, I stood up and ran into the house before anyone could come to my aid. A man shouted after me, but I didn't stop. He followed me to the house and shouted at me again as I ran down the hall. Mum opened the door, wondering what all the fuss was about as I pushed past her and sat on the sofa in shock. She spoke to the man and they came into the lounge.

Although a little shaken, I was more worried that I was in big trouble for crossing the busy road. Mum checked me over and the man offered to take me to hospital. I became hysterical because I was scared that they would keep me there. I wasn't in pain. I could move my limbs with ease, so I pleaded for her to wait until Dad came home. The man was obviously not driving too fast and had just clipped me.

Dad arrived and I remember him asking me if anything hurt. He proceeded to bend my arms and legs, none of which were broken. The man was extremely apologetic as Dad showed him out. Mum was very cross with me, so I sat in silence. The doctor came to the house and gave me a thorough examination before saying I was fine. He was happy for me not to go to the hospital but insisted that I get a good night's sleep and stay indoors for a few days to recover, so Mum tucked me up on the sofa with a cup of hot chocolate.

After my ordeal, I could not help thinking: what happened to my bag of sweets?

Chapter 5

Drama Club And Brownies

I first met Angela Rodaway when she ran a drama group at St Agnes Church hall every Sunday. It had begun in 1960, and seven years later the group had performed at the first St Paul's Festival.

It had been going for thirteen years when, at the age of nine, I started going to drama club with my sisters Patsy and Elaine. I remember taking part in the festival when Angela organised a float for the drama group. Everyone was dressed in fancy costumes as we paraded around the streets to the delight of the community. She was also actively involved in women's issues; she never wore a bra, which, looking back, made me think that she might have been a feminist. Angela was also involved in setting up a women's refuge in the area with the help of Carmen Beckford MBE. Carmen was instrumental in setting up St Paul's Festival, which is still an annual multicultural celebration of communities in and around St Paul's, better known now as St Paul's Carnival. She also set up St Paul's Dance Team, along with Terry Romaine. My sisters Elaine, Yvonne and Veronica spent many years performing with the dance team around the country.

Carmen was also a community activist in race relations and a role model who supported many Jamaican women who felt they couldn't speak up. Carmen was always helping everyone in the community. Recently, artist Michele Curtis painted murals on seven prominent walls in St Paul's with portraits of the founders of St Paul's Carnival, as well as other notable community leaders. As one of the founders, Carmen appears in one of these paintings, collectively known as *The Seven Saints of St Paul's*.

After drama club, we would go to the refuge to help decorate the house before the families moved in. I became friends with some of the children while they lived in the house, to the delight of their mums. Angela, a kind woman, was also determined to keep these families safe. She also strongly believed in equality for everyone.

During drama class, she had the natural ability of putting everyone at ease. I remember her warm-up exercises where she would get everyone walking around in a free space. We would copy her style of walking or twirling around on stage, posturing in character with ease and grace. This led to everyone ad-libbing, using props to improvise or enhance their character. Andrew, who was about fifteen, was the funniest in the group. He was a natural performer that oozed confidence. Angela gave him great speaking parts that he would recite word-perfect, performing beautifully. He went on to become a professional actor.

Angela put on a production of *Anansi the Spider Man* in which I was given the part of the tar baby. It was not a speaking part, but when Anansi fought with me he stuck to my body. I remember being dressed in a black leotard and tights. For Anansi to detach himself from my grip, he had to pull himself from my grasp. Both of us had to perform a backwards flip mirroring each other and exit the stage. The stage lights faded to mark the end of the scene. In the darkness

I quietly returned to the stage and rearranged the props before making my exit. The audience gave me my own round of applause.

The Jamaican Dance Team went on to tour Europe and Jamaica, but I was much too young and not particularly interested in dance, so I became involved with Brownies instead.

Brownies

I started attending Brownies with Veronica. Brown Owl would collect us from home and walk us to the church hall in Portland Square. She would take us on exciting nature walks around the area. This was how I was able to appreciate nature in its simplest form while living in the inner city. We used to visit St Agnes Park, not only to play, but to collect leaves and acorns that had fallen from the trees as part of our nature projects. Learning about the different trees and shrubs in the various parks we visited helped us earn badges in recognition for our work. We could also earn badges for cooking, helping around the house or going to the shops for Mum.

I recalled playing there as a toddler and was able to remember the trees and shrubs that vividly captured my imagination when I was a little girl. I often thought about this when we went on nature walks with the Brownies. In the park we would play games and work towards our badges, which, once gained, Mum would sew onto our uniforms. I had several badges, though I cannot remember what they were for. On Sundays we would march along the streets in full uniform for everyone to see. I have no memory of why we did this, but I remember feeling extremely proud.

During the meetings, we recited The Brownie Guide Law, which was an oath or promise that we agreed to live up to, promising to think of others before ourselves and do a good deed every day.

We would also sing a traditional song at the end of our meeting, calling for all the children around the world to be granted peace that we may continue to carry out good deeds and stay true to ourselves.

Chapter 6

I Think I'm Going To Die

At the age of eleven, I started my period, although I didn't know exactly what a period was. No one had actually told me where a period came from, so I knew I was dying. With soggy, bloody panties I ran to my mother, who was busy making dinner in the kitchen, and wailed at her, sobbing uncontrollably, "Mum, I'm dying – I'm bleeding from my 'foo foo'."

Tears rolled down my face, soaking my undeveloped chest, as I ran to my mother and buried my head inside her floral dress. She stared at me with pity in her eyes, cupped my face in her loving hands and tilted my head to one side as she gave me her undivided attention. I continued to sob even louder, gripping my lower abdomen and rocking from side to side (because that's what women do when they're in pain – I'd seen it on the TV). I reached the point of vocal hysteria and at the same time I was able to take in several deep breaths, which I had mastered to perfection. I had rehearsed my vocal hysteria having previously been trapped by Veronica after she coerced me into a corner when no one was looking and proceeded to pull my hair, punch me in the arm or kick me in the leg – whichever took her fancy. She would only stop when I pleaded to my mother to help me.

On this occasion, I was still sobbing as Mum left the room and I saw the opportunity to stick my fingers inside my mouth and load the ends with spittle, which I then dabbed on my already sodden cheeks.

Mum returned to the kitchen, smiling sweetly, holding a long and obscene-looking bandage and said in her broad West Indian accent, "Put it inside yu drawers."

Confused and horrified at the thought, I protested and said, "If I'm dying, I want my Teddy." I cried a little harder, even though my tears had dried up. "No, Mum," I insisted. "I'm dying."

"No, it's alrite. Yu start yu period. It's puberty." And she ushered me out of the kitchen from under her feet.

Almost in an instant I stopped crying and, armed with this enormous bandage, retreated into the bathroom, softly closing the door behind me. While hovering over the toilet, I stepped out of my soggy pants and positioned the bandage under my 'foo foo', but as I started walking it dislodged itself and fell onto the floor.

"Mum!" I shouted.

She knew instantly, came to the bottom of the stairs and shouted, "Go fine anudda pair a drawers an it won't move."

I hobbled awkwardly towards my bedroom, which I shared with my older sister Patsy, and with my bandage still intact started rummaging through a pile of neatly folded clothes lying on her bed. There in among her smalls were a lacy black pair of pants, which I carefully pulled from the pile and shook free before stepping into them. Still clenching my knees, I pulled the silky pants over the cheeks of my bottom, careful not to dislodge the bandage. Once in place, I awkwardly hobbled towards her bed and retreated under the comfort of the sheets, feeling relieved that I wasn't dying after all. With Teddy in my arms, I told him everything was going to be alright. After all, it

47

was only puberty and I wasn't going to die. We snuggled up together and I slowly drifted off into a deep sleep.

I shared a bedroom with Patsy until she left home. Prior to leaving school, she was well into fashion and began making all her own clothes. She loved the fashion of the '50s and could run up a skirt or dress in no time at all. It was not unusual for her to disappear into her bedroom with a cup of hot chocolate and a packet of ginger nut biscuits, only to appear later smiling and holding her latest creation, ready to wear out that evening. Being in the same room, I was the first to see all her creations.

I went shopping with her most Saturdays to Debenhams, where she would spend ages looking through all the *Vogue* patterns, fabrics, zips or buttons to go with a new outfit. We also spent hours in town visiting every shoe shop, which used to annoy me because we would end up going in circles, then she would purchase the first pair she had tried on. She accessorised all her outfits with gloves, costume jewellery, a clutch bag and a fur coat. She wore Biba or Mary Quant make-up and would never leave the house without wearing her lipstick.

Her friends from school, Pauline and Carol, were also keen on fashion. They had similar taste in clothes but would try to outdo each other with the garments they wore. It was the simple things they created that made them unique. I remember Patsy came home from work with several black T-shirts plus a bag of white letters. Armed with the iron and board, she disappeared into her bedroom, then transferred the letters onto each T-shirt to display the different captions 'Big Youth', 'Jah!' (God) and 'Rastafari'. Another time she bought a pair of black gloves; not satisfied with the look, she sewed numerous sequins across the knuckles for more effect. Patsy continues to be a unique creator of colourful arts and fashion.

Keith was good with his hands. Together with his friends, they spent hours building bicycles by using old frames in the garden.

Once they built a go-cart using the frame of an old pram, then took it in turns to race along the side streets. Any spare bits were never wasted but ended up on the floor in his bedroom. When he and his friends were not making things, they'd often be bickering about such things as a catapult that someone had broken. He was also a member of The Boys' Brigade and could play the bugle. Every week he visited St Gabriel's Church at the top of the road to practise. When the Scouts or Boys' Brigade were on parade, they would march around the streets en route to the church and the family would go to the Sunday service to support my brother. The church had the most beautiful stained-glass windows so, when the lights were on, images of the disciples or the Virgin Mary holding baby Jesus shone through. However, inside the church it was cold and after early-morning mass it always smelt strongly of incense. There was a junior school attached to the church. Being so close, I'm not sure why Mum didn't change me to that school when we moved to our new house. I would have happily gone there as I knew many of the kids who attended that school.

By the time Keith was in his late teens, he was part of Enterprise Sound System (a disc jockey). This was where he, together with his friends, could play Jamaican music. The DJ would toast (sing) on the mike at the dance. Huge speakers were built to blast out heavy reggae, bass or dub music for everyone to enjoy until the early hours of the morning.

I was a member of the local library, but it was Elaine who was the bookworm. Her favourite books were Ian Fleming's James Bond series, as well as Mills & Boon. She loved boiled sweets and it wasn't unusual for her to be munching on a quarter-pound of cola cubes, Murray Mints or fruit bonbons. When she wasn't engrossed in her favourite book, she and her friend Lorna could often be found in the front room singing. They both became Christians at a young age, spending much of their time at church.

Chapter 7

Felix Road Adventure Playground

Coal mining was a major contributor to the economies of Bristol, Somerset and Gloucestershire during the 19th century. Although these mines are closed, there is still evidence of mining in the West Country, proudly displayed in the names of pubs and street names reflecting its past. Felix Road Adventure Playground was once the site of Easton Colliery, which operated from 1824 until 1911. From 1913 to 1972, the site served as a stone yard for Bristol building firm Cowlin.

In 1972 the adventure playground was established by a group of local parents concerned that their children should have a safe space to play in. Apart from the park at the top of St Gabriel's Road, it was ideal as Eastville Park was at least two miles away. It was also in a good catchment area for all the kids who lived in Easton and situated around the corner from our house. Our parents were integral in preserving a redundant space in the community as a creative play area for thousands of children, who still enjoy this space fifty years on.

My sister Elaine was thirteen when the adventure playground first opened. She said it had large iron gates, which opened onto an area of grassland. She remembers a group of young white guys with long hair, wearing flares, arriving to start work on building the new structures out of wooden planks, telegraph poles and rope, together with anything else they could lay their hands on. They came to our house and Mum gave them cups of tea. I can only imagine that happened because Mum had been involved from the start and they had become friends, such was her character – a kind person who would help anyone.

For me, having an adventure playground nearby meant that I could play freely in my own way, in my own time, with no rules or hierarchy that I had to adhere to. Everyone who played there contributed to the build and shaped the environment according to their own vision. Apart from the play workers, adults remained absent in our play space, so for me it was special. I was very much a loner outdoors. I loved how the secure environment of the adventure playground made me feel, enjoying my own company as it gave me a feeling of independence and a total sense of freedom. I could also run, jump, crawl and skip around the apparatus, together with other kids, and be as feral as the next one. It was up to me who I gave permission to join me in my little world. Of course, Paulette was one such person.

I was about seven years old when I first played there. In the early days of its opening, I would go there with either Elaine or Yvonne and they would look after me. We spent every weekend as well as all the school holidays playing at the adventure playground, often staying out all day, losing all track of the time. It wasn't unusual for one of the kids in our street to tell us that our mum was looking for us. As we filed into the house, starving and looking rather grubby, Mum would be cursing us, saying that our dinner was getting cold. She would always finish by saying "Dat dam Vencha playgroun."

I would sit quietly at the table and allow my sisters to take the flack.

By the time I was ten, Mum allowed me to visit the 'Vench' or the 'Ventures', as it fondly became known, on my own. To begin with, I would have to return home for lunch and at teatime. By the time the summer holidays came, I was growing in confidence and becoming more independent. Yvonne had introduced me to Paulette. It turned out that her older sister, Sharon, and Yvonne went to the same school. They knew that we would be going to the same school, too. We were introduced at the Ventures and became great friends. As the days drew out and the evenings became lighter, it was a common occurrence for me to stay out all day. It was not unusual for me to leave home at 10am, often staying at the Ventures until 8pm when the adventure playground closed. My siblings came and went throughout the day, so I knew they would tell Mum that I was still out playing. When I finally arrived home, she would be cursing me as I got through the door, demanding to know where I had been. "At the Ventures playing with Paulette" was always my reply. Being the youngest, I always got away with so much more. She never grounded me. I think she knew I was at my happiest outdoors, away from her watchful eye and my squabbling siblings.

On the weekend we all had different chores to do in the house. Mine was sweeping down the stairs. If I had finished my chores and had my breakfast, Mum was happy for me to go out to play. There were times when my siblings hadn't done their chores, so everyone was grounded until all the housework was done. It was so painful having to wait for everyone to do their bit as the time dragged so slowly.

I remember waking up early on Saturdays with only one goal: to finish my chores so that I could go out to play. I was forever waiting patiently for my sisters to surface and start theirs. Yvonne was responsible for doing the weekly shopping; she also helped Mum with the cooking during the week. Patsy was responsible for cleaning the kitchen, so it fell to Elaine and Veronica that they had to clean the bathroom and living room between them. Keith would make himself scarce, then slip out of the house when no one was looking. He got away with murder as he was the only boy in the house.

One morning, having woken up early, I began to grow impatient. As no one else was up, I cleaned the stairs, kitchen and bathroom before everyone woke up. So, by the time everyone had come downstairs, the house was clean. Mum was delighted, so I could go out to play. I soon realised that if I got up early and did all the housework, Mum would let me go out to play – and it worked. If I was hungry, I would go home early, but most of the time I stayed out until the early evening. Mum knew how important the Ventures was to me, how I loved the feeling of freedom, therefore, I was never at home on time. My siblings were constantly telling me that Dad was asking where I was. This was either because I was never in when he came home from work or that I was in trouble and going to get a beating. When it was the latter, I would make sure to be home early. If Dad had arrived home before me and I saw his works vehicle parked at the top of the road, I would open the door and sit inside. Back then, no one locked their cars or front door. Eventually he would appear and I would get out of the car. The conversation would go something like this…

"Where yu cumin from?"

"Alright, Daddy. I've been to the Ventures, but I've been sat in the car waiting for you. I needed to tell you something."

I would then proceed to tell him that I had cleaned the house from top to bottom without the help of my sisters. Or that one of them had beaten me up. That was a common occurrence because I was always telling tales.

He would listen intently, then say, "Hmm, alrite, gwan inside."

My plan invariably worked and I avoided the threatened punishment. I would wave him off as he drove towards the pub at the end of the road before I went into the house. If anyone said that I was in trouble, I would never tell them I had spoken to Dad or ratted on them. Mum continued to dish out her threats, but I never took heed.

Chapter 8

The Exploding Toilet

During the summer holidays, the Ventures was my regular stomping ground. Once I had eaten my breakfast and finished my household chores, I would run out to meet my friends. Although it opened at 10am every day, I would arrange to meet my friend Paulette at 12 noon, which gave her enough time to finish her chores before meeting me. She was half my size, wore blue National Health Service glasses and suffered from an incurable illness called sickle cell anaemia, which is a blood disorder prevalent in Afro-Caribbean and Asian people. However, her poor health didn't stop us from getting into all sorts of mischief. Paulette was a very determined person and she would never let anything stand in her way.

Originally, there had been no toilets at the Ventures, but Paulette and I just happened to be there when two new Portaloos were being delivered. They were green on the outside and grey inside. They smelt strongly of disinfectant, which the delivery man said was for hygiene. We didn't know what hygiene meant, but it was up to us to ensure everyone knew that. We decided it was best that we were the first to christen one of the new toilets, so together we entered the cubicle and took it in turns to have a wee. To save our modesty, we both pretended to inspect the interior walls when it was the other girl's turn.

Once she had finished and quickly pulled up her pants, Paulette said, "Your turn," before changing positions and I did the same. Happy that everything was in order, we were now content for the other kids to use the Portaloo.

As time went by, the Portaloo became a good hiding place, particularly for games of hide-and-seek. On a sweltering hot summer's day Paulette and I took refuge inside and waited. I noticed that there was a small gap for air circulation at the bottom of the Portaloo door. Not wishing to be discovered, I convinced Paulette it was a good idea for us both to lock ourselves inside and stand on top of the toilet, just in case someone looked under the gap. Within a few minutes, the boys were outside looking for us. We remained very quiet and still for what seemed like hours. The Portaloo was becoming unbearable with the stench and the heat. It was beginning to feel like a very smelly, hot sauna so I reached for the door, but Paulette shook her head and whispered, "One more minute."

With beads of sweat rolling down our faces, we desperately needed to get some fresh air into our lungs as the smell of the 'hygiene' or disinfectant was overpowering us. We could hear the boys chattering outside. In their disappointment of not discovering us, they decided to give up. Result! Or so I thought; we hadn't been discovered. I smiled at Paulette and signalled for her to open the door. As she shifted her weight on top of the plastic seat, it cracked and then exploded in front of our very eyes as it could no longer take the weight of both of us.

The shitty contents of every kid in the area oozed out onto the floor, filling the small space with stinking, toxic fumes. We were in serious trouble and I couldn't help but retch and swear obscenities at Paulette while screaming at her to open the door. She struggled with the lock and, in desperation, I began kicking at the bolt on the door, but it wouldn't open. The stench was now intolerable as the shit and toilet paper slowly seeped under the gap of the door.

The boys, who I thought had given up searching, were in fact still outside, laughing at us. They began rocking the Portaloo violently, trying to overturn it with us inside. I began screaming and thought, Mum's going to kill me if I go home smelling all shitty. Then the door to the Portaloo burst open. Paulette took the opportunity to jump ship, while I remained stuck on the ledge.

I was still swearing profanities at her. The disgusting smell, together with the fumes of the disinfectant, made me feel dizzy and I almost passed out. A breath of fresh air reached under my nose and roused me enough to take quick action. I jumped clear from the seeping shit and landed on the hard concrete floor just beyond its reach. Relieved and gasping for air, I was about to beat a hasty retreat and make myself scarce when I noticed Paulette had been apprehended by Frank, one of the play leaders. He was none too pleased. After much pleading and protesting that the boys had barricaded the door, he accepted our story, but not before making us hose down the mess of lumpy, stinking shit as punishment for our sins.

Chapter 9

What Is That Lump?

Why is it that things always go wrong during the summer holidays? I woke up early one morning and raced to the bathroom, desperate for a wee. Hoisting my nightie high above my waist, I plonked myself down onto the toilet with only seconds to spare before having an accident. Relieved, I remained seated for a moment, glad that I hadn't wet the bed. In the past, I had been known to have a little accident while dreaming I was on the toilet, waking up to find my sheets saturated. It was always during the winter months when it was dark and bitterly cold outside. Mum had warned me about feeling the back of her hand if I was lazy enough to wet the bed again. So, when that warm sensation started, I had learned to jump out of my bed and run to the bathroom to relieve myself.

After a thorough wash of sprinkling water over my face, removing the sleep from the corners of my eyes with my fingers, washing behind my ears with any old flannel, brushing my teeth with whichever toothbrush came to hand, I was in a happy mood. That day I decided to wear my red, white and blue Jubilee socks, which my friend Linda Bennett had given me. She had giggled with pleasure, telling me that she had stolen them from Woolworths. What's more, if I didn't tell anyone, next time she would get me a pair of gunmetal grey tights.

So, true to my word, until today I have never told a soul. I decided to colour-coordinate and wear a white, tight-fitting T-shirt, which matched my socks, and a red pair of slacks.

While admiring myself in the mirror, I noticed something strange poking out on the left side of my chest. It definitely wasn't there yesterday. Tentatively, I turned to the right, but there was no lump there. I broke out into a cold sweat, swallowed hard and, with trembling fingers, explored my chest. There was a neat little lump, bulging out for all to see. How extraordinary. It couldn't be mine. How did it happen? This wasn't normal. So, having visited the doctor on my own before for dressing changes when I had stitches taken out of my knee, I saw no reason to bother Mum and decided that the next available appointment with Dr Drake had my name on it. I knew that whatever the problem was with my titty she would sort it. Paulette and the Ventures would have to wait as I had more important things to be concerned about. Off I went to see the doctor.

It was now or never; there was no going back. The titty had to go and then I could get back to normality.

The reception for the surgery was busy. I gave my name to the receptionist, who told me to go into the waiting room. I sat with all the other sick people as the doctor called out names. Glancing down at my chest, I saw the titty protruding through my top. Awkwardly, I folded my arms, hoping that no one had noticed the single lump.

"Beverley Douglas," a deep voice bellowed out over the loud-speaker. Now everyone in the waiting room knew I was seeing the male doctor. How could I tell him about the titty? For as long as I could remember in the past, I had always seen the lady doctor. My heartbeat began to increase as I slowly rose out of the chair. I wish

Mum was here, I thought. Biting down hard on my lip, I clenched my fists as I walked along the dimly lit narrow corridor to the consulting room.

Standing outside the closed door, I began to tremble. With a gentle tap, I waited but there was no answer. I sighed, released the handle, pushed opened the door and walked inside. The doctor pointed to a large leather chair opposite his desk. I nervously sat down, waiting for him to speak. Adjusting my position, I slid further into the slippery seat and grabbed hold of the armrest, careful not to fall onto the floor. I steadied myself and crossed my legs. He looked on while shuffling the papers on his desk and smirked at me. Flushed with embarrassment, I folded my arms across my chest.

"How can I help you, my dear? Is Mum outside?"

I mumbled and shifted in the chair once more, ignoring his question about Mum.

"I have a lump in my titty and it wasn't there yesterday."

There, I'd said it. Feeling even more embarrassed, I fixed my eyes to the floor. He smiled and twisted a little in his seat.

"Oh, are you in pain?"

"No, it's fine. It wasn't there yesterday."

This conversation was proving more difficult by the second and I was feeling even more uncomfortable. Sensing my unease, he picked up the phone and spoke to someone on the other end.

"The nurse is waiting for you in the treatment room and she's going to have a look at you."

Smiling, he replaced the receiver and, in my delight, I smiled back at him. I couldn't get out of the slippery chair fast enough. I bade him farewell, quick-marched out of his room and headed in the direction of the treatment room.

"And bring your mother next time!" he shouted.

I was now halfway down the corridor but ignored him, thankful that I didn't have to answer any more of his embarrassing questions. I sat in the waiting room, but I didn't have to wait long before the nurse opened the door and ushered me into her room. I could smell the disinfectant and I began to feel queasy and a little dizzy, as it reminded me of that fateful day in the Portaloo at the Ventures. I stood up and was about to make my excuses to leave, but the nurse told me to lift up my top. How did she know?

She glared at the titty for what seemed like an eternity and asked, "Have you started your period?"

Horrified, I nodded yes.

"You've started puberty."

"So, what about the titty?" I asked in desperation.

"Oh, that's all part of puberty. The other one will come out soon."

She smiled, patted my shoulders reassuringly and opened the door before ushering me out into the hallway, softly closing it behind me.

Still none the wiser as to how the other titty would come, I left the clinic, happy in the knowledge that I was not going to die for the second time in my short life.

Chapter 10

The Day I Stole The Potatoes

It was a cold winter's evening and a glowing fire lit up the night sky at the Ventures. It was unanimously decided that, as I lived closest, I should go home and return with enough potatoes for everyone to bake on the fire.

Dad was at the table eating his dinner when I arrived home. I bade him a good evening, sat by his side and waited for him to leave me some of his dinner. It was his favourite: ackee and saltfish with yam, green bananas, plantain and dumplings. Once he had eaten enough, as predicted, he slid the plate across the table, smiled and watched me as I gobbled the remainder of his dinner. I was so pleased that Paulette's sister Sharon wasn't there, otherwise, Dad would have given her his plate because he knew that I'd already eaten. Belly full, I retreated into the kitchen with the empty plate and then I remembered the potatoes.

Filling my pockets from the big sack of King Edward potatoes, I shuffled out of the kitchen into the lounge. Dad was dozing on the sofa. As I cleared its top end and reached for the door handle, I heard a loud thud. A large potato slowly rolled towards his head. There was a stifled laugh from Mum and a huge gasp from my sister Patsy. I froze and thought it best to leave that potato behind, and continued opening the door. I thought that if I ignored the potato Dad wouldn't see me as I had my back to him and I couldn't see him either.

In his deep West Indian voice, he asked very calmly, "Where yu goin wid dat potato?"

Caught red-handed, I froze on the spot. "To the Ventures."

"Put dem rite bak, evry las one."

Very slowly, I turned around to face everyone and another potato rolled out from in between my knees. Mortified at being caught, I had no choice but to put them all back. Dad ushered me out of the living room and I closed the door behind me to the sound of hysterical laughter.

I returned to the Ventures to a frosty reception, but when I relayed my dilemma everyone roared with laughter and I was forgiven.

Chapter 11

Bollywood In The Making

It was a cool summer's evening and the Ventures had closed. As usual, Paulette and I were impatiently waiting for the coast to be clear before we climbed over the gate and sneaked into our special place. The daily ritual of hoisting her over the gate was gradually getting more difficult as she was becoming heavier and I had almost dropped her the previous evening. She still wasn't best pleased with me and muttered something under her breath as I sheepishly clambered to the top of the gate and straddled my legs either side of it. Once in position, I leaned down towards her and held out my hand for her to grab hold of, so she could pull herself up. Instead, she yanked my arm towards her, almost pulling me off the gate, and threw me the deadliest of glares.

"You better not drop me."

I nodded at her and, feeling under pressure, I began to pull her up towards me. I couldn't understand why she had suddenly gained those extra pounds. Then it dawned on me. Earlier she had filled up a plastic bottle with water and concealed it inside her jacket – heaven only knows why she needed a jacket in this heat. We were almost over the gate when I noticed that we were being watched.

Our antics were amusing the little roly-poly Indian boy. I immediately recognised him as his father owned the corner shop not far from Paulette's house. I slowly lowered her back down to the ground, joining her and the roly-poly Indian boy.

She was just about to curse me out when he asked, "What are you doing?"

"It's none of your business," replied Paulette.

"Can I come into the Ventures with you?"

"Well, you'll have to give us some sweets first."

"I don't have any sweets right now, but I can get some tomorrow."

Happy with his promise, we shook hands, knowing that he couldn't go back on his word, otherwise, he'd be in real trouble. Neither of us had made threats like this before, but we had a whole day to decide on a punishment for him. Suddenly I had an idea and whispered into Paulette's ear. She was delighted and started to chuckle as we both circled him.

"Can you dance?" I asked as sheer horror came over his face and his knees began to wobble, which amused us even more.

"Yes, but not without music," he said.

"Well, I'll be the treble and you do the bass, Cutie," Paulette replied.

I had no idea what she was talking about, but I nodded in agreement. I only knew the songs that we sang in church, but I was definitely up for the challenge. She cleared her throat, then retrieved the bottle of water from under her jacket. She unscrewed the top and took a swig, before wiping the nozzle and handing it to me. I did the same. The roly-poly Indian boy stretched out his hand and Paulette simply said, "After". She replaced the top, positioning the bottle between her feet.

After a count of three, she raised both hands to her mouth, cupped them together and started making noises. I did the same and blew raspberries, which saturated the insides of my hands. Paulette's eyes lit up as she nodded her head and grinned at me. She loved it. When the rhythm was to her liking, she nodded to the roly-poly Indian boy to start dancing. With both arms raised to his waist, he mimicked a jive and wobbled from side to side. It was hysterical, but I dared not stop through fear of being cursed. Tears rolled down my face and, unable to contain my amusement any longer, the two of us looked at each other and erupted into hysterical laughter.

Slapping him on his back and wiping my sodden hands on his T-shirt, we congratulated the roly-poly Indian boy for passing his initiation test and allowed him to become the first member of our gang. As promised, Paulette rewarded him with a sip of water and, together, we hoisted her up high and pushed her over the gate. Once inside the Ventures we enjoyed getting to know our new friend Ranjit Singh.

It turned out that Paulette and Ranjit went to the same school. He was in the year below her, but they had not spoken until the day he caught us climbing over the gate at the Ventures. The corner shop that his dad owned was not far from where Paulette lived and she often saw Ranjit stacking the shelves.

Once our friendship grew, she called for him at the shop while he was working, but his dad didn't approve, asking her, "If he is out playing with you, who will stack my shelves?"

Ranjit was embarrassed and said that it was probably best if she didn't call for him while he was helping his dad. He would eventually join us much later in the day, bearing gifts of Spangles or Polo Fruits sweets, which we were grateful for. He was only allowed out for a few hours each day before having to return home, so we made the most of our time together.

Ranjit had few friends and some of those he did have bullied him or made fun of him because he was overweight. He suffered with asthma and used an inhaler, which made it difficult for him to run around or play football with the other boys. Whenever he became short of breath, he would take himself off somewhere quiet to puff on his inhaler. If I saw him heading off, I would follow him and sit quietly beside him until he felt better.

In time, he preferred to hang around with us and was glad to make mischief with us. He sometimes got on my nerves as he was a real chatterbox, always talking about the latest boys comic that had arrived in his dad's shop, which was of no interest to me. However, he had a great sense of humour, which I put down to all the rubbish that he read in his comics. In truth, he was very gentle. Both Paulette and I had a soft spot for him. He was often helpful and he proved to be useful when we were collecting firewood. It was also handy having him around when I needed to pull Paulette over the gate after the Ventures had closed. Sadly, he never got to experience the joys of sharing the fire with us or my roasted potatoes as he always had to go home early.

We missed Ranjit when he disappeared for several weeks during the summer holidays, but soon learned that he had gone to India to visit his grandparents. He told us about the festival of Holi or festival of colour, which is centred around the burning and destruction of the demoness Holika, which lasted for days. He said the fun part was being covered with coloured powder that everyone threw at each other, as well as squirting water guns.

Chapter 12

The Day I Lost My Cherry

There were several fun haunts close to the Ventures and Bannerman Road Primary School was a favourite. It was close to the railway bridge and a short distance from both our homes. Paulette attended the school and was familiar with its surroundings, particularly the two large cherry trees that were within its boundaries. Since the spring, she had kept a watchful eye on their changes, regularly reporting back to me on how the cherries were forming and taking pride of place among the pink petals. She told me her master plan was for me to scale the six-foot wall, crawl along the top and climb onto the branches of the cherry tree. She in turn would wait at the bottom and catch the cherries as I carefully threw them down to her. Laden with our feast, we would go off to the field next to the school and scoff the lot.

By the time the school holidays were upon us, the cherries were juicy-red, ripe for picking, but there was only a week's window to strip the trees bare. We sat outside the school grounds at different times of the day, observing people passing by. Around the early evening, the traffic got quieter so I was sure we wouldn't be discovered. We arranged to meet at 6pm when most of the kids had gone home for tea, so at the allotted time I made my way to the school.

As I got closer to the school, I saw Paulette was already there.

"Alright, Paulette?"

"Come on," she replied impatiently as I dutifully handed her the small, crumpled brown paper bag, which I had brought from home. She was not amused and screwed it up and threw it to the ground. I watched in silence as she pulled out a large plastic carrier bag from inside her coat pocket and handed it to me.

"You just said bring a bag, so that's what I did," I said.

She thrust the bag in my direction and not fazed by her rudeness, I grabbed it, tucked it inside my pocket for safekeeping and smiled to myself. I too had a cunning plan. I approached the wall and clambered on the top to survey the best point to begin my ascent into the cherry tree. Being that high up, the wind howled through the branches and shook the leaves, making it difficult for me to keep my balance. Careful not to fall and humiliate myself, I held on tight and continued climbing until I reached the highest point of the tree. I positioned my feet onto the smaller branches and, happy that they would take my weight, rested my back on a solid piece of trunk. There in front of me was an abundance of beautiful red cherries glistening in the sun.

With my hands shaking and my mouth salivating, I very carefully plucked one from a small bunch. Ready for eating and with not a moment to spare, I popped it into my mouth. The cherry immediately exploded on my tongue, sending a deliciously sweet sensation down the back of my throat. I reached for several more, greedily stuffing them into my mouth and closed my eyes, savouring that moment of pure indulgence. Down below a weak voice broke the silence as Paulette's voice reminded me that I had a job to do.

Quickly throwing the stones into the school grounds, I popped several more cherries into my mouth before shaking the branches and watched a few overripe ones fall to the ground. I smiled to myself as I watched Paulette picking them up and wiping the dirt off before she ate them, too. At least that would keep her quiet for a while. I stripped the tree bare and filled the bag almost to the top. I must have picked a good three pounds in weight. With the wind still howling, I carefully lowered the bag down to Paulette and began to make my descent when suddenly she shouted, "Stop! Don't come down yet! You've left one." She pointed up at the tree.

I was sure that I had stripped it bare. I followed her directions and surveyed the tree once more. To my annoyance, she was right. There, just out of reach, hidden behind a cluster of leaves was the biggest, juiciest, most succulent-looking cherry winking at me. I only caught sight of it when the breeze parted its leaves. How on earth did she see it from where she was standing, especially when she was the one wearing glasses? But, more to the point, how was I going to reach it? The branches at the far end of the tree were very thin and I was sure even a cat would have thought twice about taking the risk.

Paulette, on the other hand, was having none of it. Even when I protested, she refused to leave the last succulent cherry behind. It was times like this that I wished I could stand up to her; well, maybe one day. Having secretly eaten so many cherries, I was feeling rather full and a little queasy. All I wanted to do now was go into the playing fields next to the school, lay on my back with the warmth of the evening sun on my face and relax. But that wouldn't be until I had picked that last cherry. With a deep sigh, I carefully crawled along the branch towards my final prize. Stretching outwards along the thin branch, I could almost touch it. Suddenly, the branch started to bend downwards as I desperately tried in vain to scramble backwards to safety. The weight of my body tore through each branch, snapping them clean off as I crashed noisily through the tree, frantically grabbing at anything in sight to break my fall.

With all the rigorous shaking of the tree, the luscious cherry fell from the branches and tumbled towards Paulette. After what seemed like ages, I crashed out of the tree and landed heavily on my left side, jarring every bone in my body, causing me agonising pain. Winded and catching my breath, I lay motionless as I watched Paulette grab the bag of cherries and erupt into hysterical laughter. She danced around me, oblivious to how badly I was hurt. Unable to move, let alone speak, tears filled the corners of my eyes and rolled down the sides of my cheeks. My spirit completely broken, I sobbed uncontrollably.

Eventually, she managed to compose herself and, realising I was hurt, knelt down beside me and whispered in my ear, "Did you get the cherry?"

I glared at her and slowly rolled onto my back as the feeling in my side started to return. While I cradled my arm (which I was convinced was broken), she placed her arm comfortingly around my shoulder and helped me to sit up. Without warning, she let out a loud scream.

"Oh my God, you're bleeding."

I immediately pushed my injured arm up in the air, forgetting how painful it was, quickly dropping it to my side again. "Where?"

Looking down at my wounded arm and feeling a little sheepish, I said, "No, Paulette, I've just crushed my cherry." Feeling extremely nauseous, I stumbled to my feet. With dented pride, I bade Paulette farewell and hobbled in the direction of home.

"What about your share of the cherries?"

"Keep them," I replied. Without turning back, I limped off home.

Chapter 13

My First Driving Lesson

Dad was always tinkering with cars instead of paying out for expensive garage bills and spent hours under the bonnet of his blue and white Austin Cambridge motor car. The interior seats and steering wheel cover were made of black leather. The dashboard was made of walnut and the horn had a red crest in the centre. At the rear, on the boot, the Austin logo took pride of place. I loved watching as he fiddled around with the greasy spark plugs and shock absorbers, and as beads of sweat trickled down his forehead as he tightened the nuts and bolts. A final tap and blow over the parts appeared to free them of dust. Content, Dad would hum and whistle familiar tunes while smoking his Capstan Full Strength cigarettes. Taking the last puff of his cigarette, he would start up the engine and a final adjustment usually did the trick on the old girl, as he called the car. It was as good as new. Then came the test drive. He would get into the driver's seat, wind down the window and shout, "Yu cumin?"

I didn't have to be asked twice as I loved any excuse to go for a drive, so I would scramble off the wall and join him. Eagerly, I watched him depress the brake pedal, put it into gear and release the handbrake. The old girl would splutter and off we went. I was so proud of my dad; he could do anything.

On one particular day, having only travelled a short distance, I noticed plumes of black smoke belching out of the exhaust. The old girl was on fire, or so l thought. Dad pulled over to the kerb and the old girl came to an abrupt halt. Cursing and swearing under his breath, he opened the bonnet, removed his oily rag from inside his pocket and wiped his sweaty brow while looking baffled.

To say that I was disappointed our journey had been cut short was an understatement. All I could do was sigh in disbelief and sit back in the hope that the old girl would start again. How could I make Paulette jealous now, when I had only travelled a few hundred yards? I had already planned on telling her that we had travelled along the new dual carriageway at sixty miles per hour, knowing that she would be green with envy as her father didn't own a car.

"Is the car going to start again, Daddy?"

Looking perplexed, he mopped his brow again with his oily rag, lit another cigarette and said, "I don't know, Spallydew."

Lord only knows where he got my nickname. Most girls are called Princess or Pumpkin, but the Jamaicans are priceless when it comes to nicknames. I did like being called Cutie, which was how my family and the kids at the Ventures referred to me.

"I tink I need sum elp dis time. Gwan ome an get yu bredda an sistas."

What on earth for? was my initial thought, but dutifully I did as I was told and, leaving the comfort of my seat, ran the short distance back to the house. I flung open the front door, gasping for breath, before spluttering out the awful predicament Dad had found himself in. Unimpressed, Mum rolled her eyes and shouted for everyone to go with me and help Dad. Through stifled tuts and objections, one by one my siblings followed me. Keith protested the loudest, so Mum gave him a swift slap around the ear, which immediately silenced him. A chorus of hysterical laughter echoed in the hallway as we left the house. I knew there would be trouble and Keith would seek his revenge.

As we approached the old girl, Dad was frantically turning over the engine, but she had given up the ghost. It was serious. Dad said the only option was to put her inside the council garage on the other side of the dual carriageway, where he could fix her away from the main road and out of the glare of the local bobby, who would only ask awkward questions. But how would he do that without being able to drive her there?

Puzzled, we all looked on until Dad told us that with everyone's help we could push the old girl to the garages. In agreement, I smiled at him and nodded at my siblings. Dad was amazing. I ran towards the passenger door, prised it open and proceeded to get into the passenger seat once more.

Dad got into the car beside me, glanced in my direction and said, "No, Spallydew, yu need fi elp push."

I threw him a puppy-dog look, but he just said, "Out."

Hysterical laughter erupted outside until Dad shouted at everyone to concentrate, interrupting their joviality. He gave us instructions for what to do and, disappointed, I took my place at the rear of the old girl and stood in the middle next to Veronica. She took great pleasure in whispering in my ear, "Good," and proceeded to pinch me hard on the arm. I cried out so loud the whole street could hear me. Keith came to my rescue, pulling her hair to settle the score. Content, I poked my tongue out at her and gratefully smiled at Keith, knowing that for the time being he had forgotten about us all laughing at him when Mum slapped him around the ear. In a final attempt, Dad tried to start the car again and, when she wouldn't start, he called out through the open window.

"Readi?"

He released the handbrake and, slowly, the old girl began limping away from us.

"Keep pushin an don't stop."

"Easy for you," said Veronica sarcastically.

I thought pushing the car was great fun, but I erred on the side of caution and kept quiet as I didn't want to be on the receiving end of another battering from my sister.

As we turned into Felix Road, some of the neighbours were standing gossiping on their doorsteps and chuckled at the sight of us six kids trying to push a car. I felt very proud, but by the look on my siblings' faces, it was clear that they were all dying of embarrassment. Veronica glared at me and I knew by the fearsome look on her face that she wasn't happy. To lighten the tension, I offered her a weak smile but she didn't respond, so I lowered my head to the bumper and let my thoughts wander. With a slight incline in the road ahead, the old girl became increasingly more difficult to push and it was clear that we were getting nowhere fast. No matter how much Dad shouted at us again and again to keep pushing the old girl, she was far too heavy for us.

One by one, we began peeling away from the bumper and eventually stopped pushing altogether, leaving Keith to struggle while we walked alongside him. Beads of sweat appeared across his brow and he became breathless as he tried to keep the car moving.

I heard Dad apply the handbrake on the old girl and she came to an abrupt halt, causing Keith to stumble into the bumper. Stifled laughter erupted from us, but we were silenced as he glared at each of us in turn. Dad got out of the car and joined us as we all protested that the old girl was too heavy for us. Scratching his head, he lit another cigarette and contemplated his dilemma.

"I'll drive it, Dad," said Keith.

"No, son, yu too evy, an mi need all di strent at di bac a di car."

74

"They're not pushing, Dad."

We all glared at Keith in astonishment for squealing on us.

He'd pay for that later, I thought.

Dad scratched his head again in dismay at us and puffed away on his cigarette. We watched on as he moved to the rear of the car and opened the boot. He reached inside and pulled out an old picnic blanket, rolled it up into a ball and returned to the driver's side once more, placing the blanket inside.

"Spallydew."

Dad beckoned me over to him and I was wary that I was about to be scolded for not trying hard enough. With fingers crossed for good measure, I slowly walked towards him. Behind me, I could hear my sisters muttering that I was for it now and it was all Keith's fault.

Nervously, I said, "Yes…Daddy."

"Can yu drive?"

"Yes, Daddy, yes, Daddy," I shouted, while dancing around him in the relief that I was not about to be scolded.

He turned and walked towards the driver's door and I dutifully followed him. Lifting my small frame into the driver's seat, he perched me high on top of the folded blanket to the horror of my siblings who looked on. He instructed me to hold onto the steering wheel and steer the old girl, keeping her away from the kerb. I nodded in disbelief at what I was hearing and grabbed the steering wheel excitedly with both hands. This was the day every girl dreamed of: her first driving lesson. All set and ready to go, Dad closed the door behind him, leaving me in charge of the old girl. I rehearsed in my mind what he had told me, remembering what to do if I went too fast: press firmly down on the brake pedal and the old girl would come to a halt.

At first, I couldn't quite reach the brake, but when I wriggled my bottom down further into the seat I could feel the brake pedal. I pressed down hard, confident that the old girl would now stop. After a short practice run, I was good to go. This was going to be easy, I thought, as I had practised driving on many occasions when I'd been shopping with Dad and opted to stay behind, alone in the car, so that I could pretend to drive the old girl. Wait until I see Paulette, I thought. She'll never believe me. And I wasn't going to let her forget what I did in a hurry. There was no way she could call me a liar as all the neighbours could see me, as clear as day, behind the steering wheel.

Dad directed us around the side streets, just in case we bumped into the local bobby. I happily steered the old girl along Felix Road, turning left into Villiers Road. This proved more difficult than I first anticipated as there was no power steering. As I approached the corner, I wasn't able to straighten the old girl up fast enough off the bend and she started rolling towards the parked cars. Shouts of "Straighten up! Straighten up!" and "Brake! Brake!" kept me on track as I fought with the steering wheel, trying to avoid crashing. Dad encouraged me with "Well done, Spallydew, well done." His encouragement kept me focused.

Turning left into Stapleton Road, my excitement grew as we approached the junction. Kensington Baptist Church was opposite and some of my friends, who were leaving Sunday school, looked on in astonishment when they saw me at the wheel of the old girl. I waved frantically, making sure they saw me, before Dad shouted at me to concentrate. I only wished Paulette could see me now.

I steered the old girl into Seymour Road, which had a bit of an uphill incline, and I could hear Dad telling my siblings to push harder. As luck would have it, a few of Keith's friends, who lived in that road, were playing football and joined in with helping to push the car. Happily, they took over from my sisters, who immediately bade a hasty retreat and disappeared in the opposite direction. The old girl started to speed up and I was now driving at a top speed of at least two miles per hour. Ahead was Warwick Road, a busy road that scared me. I stopped momentarily for the oncoming traffic and the line of cars travelling behind also waited patiently. I glanced behind me to see my new crew nodding back at me, so I knew I was doing a great job. Dad came to the window and asked me if I was OK.

"Oh yes, Daddy. Am I doing it right?"

"Yes, Spallydew," he replied before waving at the boys, signalling for them to push again.

Dad stood in the road just in case another car approached and, once I had cleared the junction, he helped to push the old girl again. She limped the short distance into Claremont Street and within a few hundred yards I could see the council garages. My heart sank as my first driving lesson was coming to an end. I pulled up in front of the dimly lit garages and Dad shouted at me to brake. He lifted me out of my seat and took the wheel while Keith opened the garage door. The boys gently pushed the old girl slowly into the darkness and, once she was inside, Dad got out of the car and closed the door behind him.

That was the last time I saw the Austin Cambridge.

Chapter 14

I Want Blonde Hair

Paulette and I arrived at the Ventures early on Saturday morning before the staff turned up. We were very excited as the local pet shop had donated two rabbits, which were being delivered that very morning. In order to get ready for them, we had spent the previous few days building a new rabbit hutch in a quiet corner. We painted it green so that it blended in with the plush flowers and natural vegetation for their new home. On the advice of Christina, the play leader, we had made a partition just in case one was male and the other female. We agreed that it was bad luck to give the rabbits names until they arrived. To guarantee first-class accommodation, we had laid a bed of straw and left plenty of food and water as we wanted the rabbits to be happy. Because Paulette and I had done most of the work, it was only right that we should name the rabbits. Despite no previous experience or knowledge of how to care for these pets, we were excited to take on the new challenge.

With the rabbit hutch all prepared, we sat with Christina on an old cable drum, which doubled up as a table, waiting patiently for them to arrive. Christina was a handsome woman with long blonde hair, very different from our own natty, Afro hair. Her face was covered in brown spots that she said she was born with. Paulette and I, however, were convinced that with such unusual colouring she must have black ancestry. We didn't realise until many years later that her brown spots were freckles. To finish her good looks, she wore silver-framed circular glasses, just like the ones John Lennon wore.

As we waited, Christina appeared happy for us to plait and twist her hair, pulling it this way and that, without complaint.

Remembering my favourite story of Rapunzel, we took it in turns wrapping her hair into a ball and reciting, "Rapunzel, Rapunzel, let down your golden hair." Positioning ourselves back to back, we released her hair and it would fall over our own hair. I was desperate to have beautiful blonde hair, but that would never be, or so I thought.

Finally, the local pet shop owner arrived with two beautiful rabbits, one white and the other grey. They lay very still in their tiny box and we were able to gently stroke their soft fur. Before he handed them over, he followed Christina to the place we had chosen for their new home and inspected the hutch. He gave us strict instructions as to how they should be looked after and insisted that Christina should call him if there were any problems. Paulette and I waited anxiously and, after some time, he smiled at us, displaying a mouthful of rotten teeth. Eventually, he nodded his approval, handed Christina the box and bade us farewell, leaving us with our new friends.

Carefully, Christina lifted the white rabbit out of the box and gently placed him into the warmth of my small hands. He was very soft and fluffy, and I drew him close to me and snuggled him into my favourite yellow woolly jumper. Not surprisingly, we called him Snowy. She then removed the grey rabbit and handed him to Paulette. He was a little smaller, but just as beautiful, and we instantly fell in love with our new friends. We decided he would be called Oscar. Slowly, we carried them the short distance to the corner of the Ventures, which would be their new home, and tenderly placed them inside the hutch. We watched closely as the rabbits nervously moved around, smelling the fresh bedding and, after a while, they began eating their food. Happy that they would settle, we left them, returning just before closing time to bed them down. We secured the hutch, ensuring the foxes wouldn't eat them, and left for the night.

As I walked home, I remembered the fun I'd had playing Rapunzel with Christina's beautiful blonde hair and I wondered how I too could have blonde hair; there must be a way. Still puzzling, I sighed and entered the house. Wanting to be alone, I headed for the privacy of my bedroom and sat on the bed to contemplate my dilemma. Staring into Teddy's eyes, hoping he might give me some inspiration, I snuggled up next to him. The floral smell of the clean bedding reminded me of the fresh smells of summer. I closed my eyes, breathed deeply, and in that moment it came to me. I'll get a wig!

Mum had one, which she kept in the suitcase on top of the wardrobe in her bedroom. Perhaps I could try it for size. Pushing Teddy aside, I ran into her bedroom, clambered onto the dressing table and reached into the suitcase. There it was – her beautiful, silky black wig, neatly packaged in a flesh-coloured stocking to keep it in shape. Unable to contain myself, I jumped off the dressing table and landed safely on the bed. I pulled off the stocking and fixed the wig on top of my sweaty head. After a few minor adjustments, I admired myself in the mirror, pouting my lips and shaking the fringe so that it fell into my eyes. I flicked my head from side to side, allowing the wig to move freely, and started to dance as I imagined I was one of The Supremes performing on stage.

My thoughts were prematurely interrupted when I heard Mum's voice at the bottom of the stairs. Panic-stricken, my heart racing, I stuffed the wig back inside the stocking, clambered onto the dressing table and put it back in the suitcase. Knowing I hadn't been discovered,

I tiptoed out of the bedroom, closing the door quietly behind me and returning to the sanctuary of my own bedroom.

Feeling very pleased with my discovery, all I had to do now was find a blonde wig so that I could pretend I was Rapunzel. I couldn't risk being caught on top of the wardrobe with Mum's wig and neither did I relish being scolded or getting the beating of my life, which my mother often threatened me with for being in the wrong place at the wrong time. Instead, I thought it best to wash and change before presenting myself for dinner. I had a ritual of always undressing from the bottom upwards. Standing on one foot and then the other, I would pull my socks off. Next, I would wriggle out of my slacks and knickers, having pulled them down below my knees. Finally, I would pull my vest and jumper over my head, dropping everything into a pile for someone else to clear up.

As I pulled my vest and jumper over my head, they became stuck as the neck of my jumper was too tight. I knew my jumper was a little small, but I couldn't part with it; after all, it was my favourite yellow jumper. Violently, I swished my head around in order to prise it off, flicking my head backwards and forwards. My jumper followed me with ease and, in that moment, I realised it was moving as freely as the wig. I wrestled a little more and pulled it from my head, quickly detaching my vest and throwing it onto the floor. Promptly, I placed my jumper back on my head again; it was perfect. At last, I had found the solution to having beautiful, long, blonde hair just like Christina's. I danced around the room excited, moving my head from side to side, and even managed to roll up the sleeves into a bun, before reciting the words of my favourite fairy tale.

"Rapunzel, Rapunzel, let down your golden hair."

Overjoyed, I could hardly catch my breath and swished my hair around once more. I was lost in the moment when my bedroom door burst open and Mum came crashing in. I froze on the spot as she launched at my head, grabbing at my jumper, ripping it from my head and saying, "Yu betta tec yu an Rapunzel's bac side downstairs bifor mi buss yu ass."

I quickly reached for my nightie on the bed and pulled it over my head. As she tucked my jumper under her arm, I shot past her and ran downstairs into the dining room, sat at the table and waited quietly to be served my dinner. Mum came into the room, glared at me and said, "Rapunzel," kissed her teeth and disappeared back into the kitchen.

Chapter 15

Circus Acrobatics

The Saturday pre-watershed television was the highlight of the week with wrestling starring Big Daddy, Giant Haystacks and Mick McManus, followed by the *New Faces* talent show, which gave the comedian Lenny Henry his first break on TV. His performance caused much excitement in our household that evening and he became the talk of the community for many months afterwards. The evening would be rounded off with *The Black and White Minstrel Show*, which is no longer televised due to its political incorrectness.

It was also 'Saturday Soup' day, when Mum would spend all day cooking her special Caribbean delight. Adding an array of aromatic herbs and spices that wafted throughout the house, she bulked the soup out with sweet potatoes, pumpkin, yams, dumplings and mutton, followed by a twist of love and affection. Patiently she would stir and taste small amounts of the soup until it was just right, then leave the large pot simmering gently on the gas stove for hours until Dad returned home from work. I could never understand how dinner was always cooked to perfection and ready to serve as soon as Dad came through the front door. We would all gobble mouthfuls of her delicious soup until our bowls were empty and our bellies full. This was real home cooking and I can still remember those amazing flavours to this day.

After dinner, Dad would settle down into his armchair and light up a cigarette and Mum would be busy in the kitchen while my siblings and I snuggled up, ready for the evening's entertainment, watching our eighteen-inch black and white television. Later the TV was changed for a colour one, so we were able to appreciate all the glitz and glamour of showbiz.

The wrestling started and Big Daddy was the first to enter the ring with his entourage. In a loud chorus we all started chanting "Easy! Easy! Easy!" while punching our fists in the air as he paraded in front of the crowd. Giant Haystacks followed and, as he entered the ring, we began to boo and hiss at his dark character. He was very aggressive and always got ticked off by the referee for his dirty wrestling. As Mick McManus made his way up to the ropes, he jumped clear of them and landed right in front of Giant Haystacks, who proceeded to punch him straight in the face. Mick fell to the ground, apparently injured, and the referee intervened immediately, sending Haystacks to his corner, pointing a warning finger at him. This was breathtaking stuff and the real wrestling hadn't even started yet. Between the three wrestlers, they always put on a brilliant performance.

For us, it was even more exciting because the wrestling took place at the Bristol Colston Hall. Not that we could ever afford to see them live, but it was nice knowing that they were just down the road. After all the introductions the commercial break came, during which time Keith would practise his moves, mimicking the wrestlers. I was usually his sparring partner and, unsurprisingly enough, never won a round as he was much bigger and stronger than me. When he got too carried away, Mum would interject and save me from being trussed up like a chicken, for which I was always very grateful. In her absence my only other saving grace came at the end of the commercial break when the baying crowds began shouting "Easy! Easy! Easy!" as Big Daddy paraded around in the ring again. Dad was never any use protecting me as he had fallen asleep in his chair. At the end of an exciting fun-packed show, we had time to stretch our legs and make hot Ribena drinks before the next one.

The *New Faces* talent show was next up and when Lenny Henry hit the stage I could hardly believe my eyes when I saw a young black man staring back at me. This was a first for me. This was groundbreaking for black people in the UK because he was the first young, black British comedian and later actor that appeared regularly on television. He was naturally talented and didn't play negative stereotypical roles. In time, he had his own show, which was unheard of for people of colour. He captured the true essence of the Jamaican way of life and was admired by people of all ages.

In total shock and unable to control my excitement, I bellowed at the top of my voice, "Mum, there's a black man on the telly!"

Dad immediately sat upright, woken from his sleeping slumber, and Mum burst into the room. We all stared at the television in disbelief and the room fell silent. You could hear a pin drop as we all watched a young, nervous Lenny Henry as he began telling jokes. My parents started laughing and, not really understanding adult humour, I joined in, too. Lenny took a bow and exited the stage, and we all applauded eagerly and watched the other acts. Everyone agreed that Lenny's act was by far the best as we waited with bated breath for the results. Tony Hatch was one of the judges and known for his harsh scoring, but to everyone's amazement he actually liked Lenny and he went through to win that show. And as they say, for Lenny Henry, the rest was history. Another commercial and there was a happy buzz in the Douglas household and time for another leg stretch.

I wasn't too bothered about missing the start of *The Black and White Minstrel Show* as the men wore black faces with large painted white lips and curly wigs. They looked ridiculous beside the white women who were dressed in glamorous dresses. The opening numbers were always about them parading around the stage together, which I found very boring. With all the racism around, it felt like they were mocking black people and I didn't appreciate that sort of behaviour, even at an early age. My dolly was more interesting, so I decided to fetch her from my bedroom.

Walking back along the landing, I noticed Keith's bedroom light was on so I called out to him, but there was no reply. Being inquisitive, I slowly pushed the door open. He immediately grabbed hold of my arm and threw me up against the wall. The sudden impact left me feeling dazed and disorientated as I slid down to the floor, but I still managed to hold onto Dolly. Before I could gather myself up and escape from his clutches, he lifted me high above his head and slam-dunked me onto the base of his single bed. This move was followed by him dropping his mattress on top of me and Dolly. With no time to say, "I submit", which would usually stop dangerous play, he jumped on top of the mattress and I was trapped between the two.

Panic-stricken and with no one to come to my aid, I managed to wriggle one of my legs out to the side until it was touching the floor. I shouted muffled cries of "I submit", but it fell on deaf ears. He grabbed hold of my leg and started wrenching it to and fro, causing me even more discomfort. Now breathing heavily, he seemed to be tiring from his rough play, so I decided to stop struggling and play dead in the hope that he might release me. With no hope of being rescued, all I could do was remain quiet and hope that he would let me go. I endured his bullish behaviour a while longer and eventually felt his grip loosen around my leg. Slowly, he pulled the mattress off me and I remained motionless, feigning unconsciousness. He gasped and leaned over me.

"Cutie. Wake up. I was only playing."

With Dolly in my hand, I opened my eyes and clocked him as hard as I could over the head. "I told you I submit."

He immediately fell to the floor, apparently wounded. Clutching Dolly, I wriggled out from under the mattress and casually stepped over his limp body, triumphant in my quest for self-defence, and returned to the lounge. With Dolly snuggled up in my arms, we continued watching *The Black and White Minstrel Show*. The lounge door opened and Keith came in, nursing the biggest fat coco (that's what we called a lump) above his right eye.

Alarmed, Mum asked, "Wot yu do to yu hed, bwy?"

"I fell up the stairs in the dark."

Everyone started laughing hysterically, except for Dolly and me, because we knew the truth. Keith refrained from playing wrestling games with me after that encounter. Maybe he thought it best to retire, just in case Dolly and me gave him another big fat coco.

Chapter 16

Olympics At The Ventures

In the summer of 1976, I was twelve years old and remember a heat-wave that caused water shortages around the country. The authorities monitored all water usage. Households were restricted to water stand-pipes, there was a hosepipe ban, the use of car washes was banned and filling a bathtub was also forbidden until the ban was lifted some weeks later.

1976 was also the year of the Montreal Olympics, which at the time didn't stir up much enthusiasm with the kids at the Ventures as it was far too hot. Unbeknown to us, Steve the play leader had arranged with Frank to hold an Olympics for all of us. They had spent weeks deciding on which events would take place and the age group for each category. To make things more competitive, we would be competing against St Paul's Adventure Playground and there would be prizes for the winners.

In time everyone, Paulette and I included, warmed to the idea and busied ourselves with the big clean-up of clearing old tyres and rotten wood around the play area. With no expense spared, new ropes for the pulley were erected, as well as new nets for the tennis court and new basketball rings to replace the old ones. Steve marked out lines for the running tracks and fresh sand arrived in a large pickup truck to fill the sandpit, ready for the high jump. All these changes made the Ventures look like a proper sports facility and plants, which had been donated by the local allotments, were placed all around to finish off our Olympic Village.

News of our Olympics travelled fast and kids from all over Easton came to practise their various disciplines to improve their chances of winning a prize. I was excited. I knew I could win some of the heats as I was pretty nimble on my feet, but the competition from the other adventure playground was unknown, so everyone was training hard. My favourite activity was the pulley and I reckoned on coming first at flying through the air at speed or running around the full area of the Ventures, knowing that no one in my age group could catch me. I also knew I could cross the tightrope faster than anyone else. Having fallen off and broken my arm during the Easter holidays, I was a little out of practice, but I was sure I could put in a good performance. The only worry was that if my mum found out I had gone back to playing on the tightrope she wouldn't allow me to take part, as she said that it was too dangerous. I swore Paulette to secrecy, promising to share my prize with her if she kept quiet.

I arrived early at the Ventures and amused myself on the tightrope and the pulley until Paulette arrived. In the distance I could see her looking around for me. I waved at her from the top of the pulley slope, catching her attention, and waited for her to join me. Eager to share the news that the Ventures would be hosting their own Olympic games, I told her that Steve had an important job for her. She listened with interest and nodded in agreement, giving me a weak smile, but I knew by the smug look on her face that she was pleased I was thinking of her. She watched me as I jerked the pulley towards me and recklessly mounted the large tyre, before whizzing down the slope at an exhilarating speed with the wind behind me. She could only look on as I repeated my descent a few more times. She was far too nervous and afraid of heights to have a go, but it didn't stop her from giving me advice on how to improve my technique.

"Why don't you come down the pulley with me?" I asked her.

"No way – it's too high and I might fall off."

"Not if I hold onto you really tight, and we could do it together. I'll get on first and you can sit on top of me. We won't go that fast with two of us on it."

"No," she repeated.

"Come on. Don't be scared. I'll hold onto you real tight."

Paulette stood firm and, for the first time, I saw a weakness in her I had never seen before. I began to make chicken noises, posturing around her.

"It's like you're flying – I know you'll love it. You only have to do it once, and if you don't like it that's fine, but at least you would have tried it."

I clambered onto the tyre and beckoned her towards me, pulling her up so that we were in close quarters and facing each other. I clasped my arms around her back and jerked the pulley.

"Hold on tight!" I shouted as the pulley sprang into action and, slowly, we started moving. Whoosh! Picking up speed, we sailed through the air. Delighted, Paulette let out a loud scream and giggled with excitement, clearly enjoying the thrill as it came to an end. She jumped off, full of joy, and laughed some more. I retrieved the rope and tyre before we walked the short distance to the top of the slope again. Just for a moment, she had forgotten about her fear of heights. Steve came and joined us and asked Paulette if she was interested in taking part in the Olympics. I immediately told him that we both were, but I would be doing all the field events.

"Do I get a prize, too?" she asked.

"That all depends how well you do your job on the day, Paulette. What do you say?"

"Alright, but I'm not doing any running."

Steve smiled at her as we set off to play again, leaving her to contemplate his proposal for her to help him during the day. Happy in the knowledge that Paulette wouldn't be left out of the Olympics, we could only wait for the day to come.

On the day of our Olympic Games the air was full of nervous excitement and expectation. Kids from all over Easton started arriving at the Ventures in the hope of taking part and winning an event. In no time, everyone was practising their disciplines.

Robert was one of the first to arrive on his red chopper bicycle. He lived at the bottom of my street, so I saw him most days. He was very tall and good-looking for his age and he stood out above all the other boys. I had a bit of a crush on him and I think our feelings were mutual as he often called for me to go to the Ventures with him. He would pick me wildflowers when no one else was around and we sometimes walked home together after a day at the Ventures. He was always smartly dressed and today was no exception. He wore a very fetching green pair of shorts with white stripes on the side, a white T-shirt and knee-high bright yellow socks that I recognised as being the same colour as those of the school football team. He parked his bicycle beside the wall before scanning the Ventures. I waved at him from the top of the slope and signalled for him to join me.

"Alright?"

"Yeh," I said, smiling at him and feeling a little flushed as I handed him the pulley.

Careful not to scuff his white plimsolls, he mounted the pulley, jerking himself to go faster before travelling at speed down the slope. As he reached the end, he crashed into the barrier and fell to the ground, lying motionless for a few seconds. I gasped and ran down the slope towards him. Before I could reach him, he stood up and dusted himself down.

"Are you alright, Robert? Are you hurt?"

Steve came running over from the clubhouse with a concerned look on his face. "I've oiled the pulley, so you need to be careful."

"Idiot," Robert replied as he clutched his arm and started to limp off towards the crowd of boys who had now gathered at the entrance to the Ventures and were scanning the area.

"Rob!" I shouted.

"I'll be fine, honest. I'll see you later."

Without another word, he was walking towards his friend Steven, who had seen him crash and was coming to his aid. The two boys embraced and I watched as they headed off into the distance.

Robert's friend Steven aka Guzoom was so named because he was a great sprinter. He too had made a special effort for the games and was sporting a white T-shirt, a multicoloured tracksuit and red socks. Naughty Norman and his posse had also arrived, all wearing white T-shirts and blue jeans, ready for the games.

In high spirits, we waited patiently for the arrival of the opposition from St Paul's Adventure Playground. Paulette arrived with her lunch for the day, which consisted of enough jam sandwiches for the both of us and a litre of Ribena squash. In my haste to arrive early at the Ventures, I had forgotten about lunch and my promise to bring some potatoes for the fire. Not wishing to be scolded for my forgetfulness, I quickly changed the subject and suggested that we locate Steve and find out what tasks she would be doing throughout the day.

While he briefed her, I slipped out the back door and joined the boys, who were anxiously waiting for the visitors. The opposition arrived in an old, battered minibus, but it was more than we had at Felix Road. They were all smartly dressed in coordinated uniforms, sporting red T-shirts, black shorts and matching tracksuits, making them look like real athletes. Steve and Frank, the officials for the day, greeted them and began organising registration for the competitors. The staff from St Paul's were also on hand to ensure the smooth running of our Olympics and that all the competitors were registered into the right event and age group for each heat. It was finally announced that there would be ten heats, which were: throwing the rounders ball; high jump; long jump; tennis; table tennis; shooting basketballs into the net; descending the pulley; 100 metres running around the Ventures; 400 metres relay running around the Ventures; and, finally, a tug of war.

At the end of each event, Paulette was given the job of running over to give the final times to the officials and also ensuring that the competitors had plenty of water throughout the day. She looked very important as she raced around wearing her yellow tabard, carrying her official clipboard.

Ranjit joined us, wearing a white T-shirt and shorts together with a white baseball cap. He looked very smart and official, too. At first Paulette was irked that he had been drafted in to help with the smooth running of the day, but I convinced her that he could prove to be helpful to her. So, she appointed Ranjit as her helper and delegated some of her tasks to him, which made her feel more important. Poor Ranjit seemed to be fetching and carrying for several of the other kids, as well as doing his own tasks.

The first event was the under-elevens field event of throwing the rounders ball; there were ten competitors in total, including me. The instructions were that the best of three throws from either a standing or running position would win. If there was a tie, we would have to throw again until there was a clear winner. It was Ranjit's responsibility to collect all the balls once everyone had taken part, then return them to the competitors before the next round. I could see him in the distance, waiting patiently.

Steve called the competitors to the line and, nervously, I waited for my turn. There were some very good throws from everyone and

I knew that it wasn't going to be easy. My name was called and I collected the ball and scanned the area where I wanted it to land. Taking a few steps backwards, I paused before running up to the line and hurled the rounders ball high into the air. It soared higher and higher before dipping and landing with a thud close to an official. Everyone gasped as it was a good first throw and I was very pleased with my effort. The official placed a marker into the ground and wrote down the distance. I looked on in anticipation as the first round came to an end. By the position of all the markers, I could see that I was in first place. Overjoyed, I skipped back to join the other competitors and smiled at my friends, who cheered loudly, and waited patiently for my second throw. The official called me for my second throw and I made my way up to the line again.

My hands were sweating, so I wiped them onto my shorts and took up my position a few feet from the line. With all my might, I hurled the rounders ball high into the air. It rotated several times before tumbling downwards and landed on the ground in among the cluster of all the other stakes. Cupping my hands over my mouth, I held my breath and waited for the result. The official danced around the stakes and measured the distance several times, before finally giving me a thumbs up signal and indicating that it was a good second throw. Everyone jumped for joy as it was close run, but it kept me in first position. I clenched my fists and smiled – not too much as the game wasn't over yet.

My friends came running towards me and patted me on the back, which only spurred me on to do better. Fingers tightly crossed, I watched as everyone performed to the highest standard. For the last time, I was called by the official to take up my position at the line. With the hot sun beating down on my forehead, beads of sweat trickled down the sides of my face. For the first time, I felt a real anxiety to win.

The crowd shouted and shook their empty ginger beer cans filled with stones and blew their whistles even louder to spur me on. "Go

Cutie, go Cutie, go Cutie!" They were making an awful racket, but it made me feel good. I took a deep breath to settle my nerves and, looking far into the distance, I focused on where I wanted the rounders ball to land. With a hop, a skip and a run up to the line, with all my might, for the last time, I hurled the rounders ball high into the air and watched it spin past the official and beyond the tape, before it fell and landed in the dust.

Everyone screamed and shouted with delight as it came to rest. Needing a longer tape, the official ran to the spot and measured the distance, which had clearly exceeded all the other competitors. With a double thumbs up everyone cheered as I was declared the winner over our St Paul's rivals. The contestants all congratulated me and I knew it was a gold medal for me.

Paulette and Ranjit were quickly on hand with more water, which I devoured quickly to quench my thirst. "Drink – you need to keep your strength up," Paulette said. Before I could say anything, Paulette, closely followed by Ranjit, went off to collect the score sheet from the officials.

The official had acquired a megaphone and started to announce the next event: the high jump, which Guzoom was the favourite to win. All ten competitors got through the first two rounds, but as the bar was raised to the next height several failed to clear it and were knocked out of the round. By round four, only three competitors were left. The official signalled for Guzoom to take his jump and everyone was confident that he would clear this height. Guzoom prepared to take his turn, rocking himself back and forth in preparation. He ran towards the bar, lengthening his stride as he got closer. With the greatest of ease, he pushed his arms high up into the air and head first he catapulted his long, slender body and dived over the bar. As he descended towards the sandpit, his foot caught the bar and it tumbled clean off its mount, to the horror of everyone.

The St Paul's kids cheered with excitement at his failure. Guzoom had landed awkwardly and appeared to be injured. With a little help from the official, he rose to his feet, clearly disappointed. He stared into the crowd and shook his head, before dusting himself off and joining the boys. I watched on as Naughty Norman and Robert took him to one side and gave him a stern talking to, pushing and prodding him in the chest to ensure he was paying attention.

"Come on, man," the boys said in chorus. "You've got two more goes at that height. You can do this, man."

Guzoom nodded in agreement before turning to watch the remaining jumps. The official signalled for Guzoom to have a second jump and he very slowly took his position. He surveyed the bar and repeatedly slapped his cheeks to put himself in the zone. A chorus of "Guzoom! Guzoom! Guzoom!" echoed around the Ventures together with the sound of whistles and ginger beer cans rattling. He ran towards the bar, leapt high into the air and glided over it, this time careful not to lower his foot too soon. He landed in the sandpit and threw his hands up in the air in triumph, smiling broadly for all to see. The crowd went wild and Guzoom took a bow before joining the boys again. They patted him on his back as he enjoyed the moment.

Round five and the bar was raised again. More competitors were knocked out and so far only one boy had managed to clear it. Guzoom was up next and he knew that he had to clear this height, otherwise he would finish in second place. In anticipation, I placed my hands over my mouth and anxiously waited. The crowd fell silent and you could hear a pin drop as we watched on. Beads of sweat slowly trickled down Guzoom's face as he jumped up and down several times, swinging his arms across his chest and rocking his head from side to side. He repeated this several times and, now completely focused, he slowly ran towards the bar, picking up speed at the last few steps. Everyone cheered as he threw his hands upwards and leapt high into the air. Head first he dived over the bar, clearing it with ease, and continued to somersault before descending and landing on his feet.

He fell to his knees and punched his fists towards the sky in triumph. Everyone rushed forwards to congratulate him while the St Paul's kids looked on in defeat. The last competitor from St Paul's knocked the bar from its mount, unable to match up to Guzoom's final jump. Everyone screamed and cheered with delight as the official declared him the overall winner.

Naughty Norman and Robert were up next, shooting basketballs in the ring, which they won with no pressure. Leonard also won the tennis. However, it didn't all go our way. The table tennis and pulley events were won by the kids from St Paul's, as well as the long jump. We would have to settle for three bronze medals in those events.

By midday, the sun was at its highest. There was little or no shade and it was proving difficult to keep cool under the sweltering heat. The competition was also heating up and everyone was feeling under pressure to do well. Steve encouraged us to drink and handed out more bottles of water, for which we were all grateful. He spoke of his concerns to the officials and suggested that the boys should be given a longer time to recover after their heats, which they agreed to.

Steve and Frank then gathered us all together for an inspirational talk. Frank said that in their eyes we were all winners and it was the taking part, not the winning, that was important. Our spirits were lifted when he told us Felix Road was slightly ahead on points, but warned that there was still a long way to go. We all applauded and cheered with delight, believing that we really could win our Olympic Games.

Paulette and Ranjit joined us, carrying a large cool box, which they handed to Frank. He removed the lid and it was filled with lots of sweets, chocolates and fizzy drinks.

"Tuck in," he said. "They'll give you the energy you need to get back into the race."

Everyone dived into the cool box and pulled out their favourite chocolates, munching away and feeling their energy levels rising.

Naughty Norman, taking the lead from Frank, added his two pennies' worth and said, "Come on, team, we'll never give up. We'll fight to the bitter end."

After the break, another official announcement called the competitors for the next race: the tightrope crossing. This was a relay where all the team had to walk across the tightrope, but you couldn't begin crossing until the contestant before you had reached the other side. The team with the fastest time would be the winner. The visitors were to go first and the official at the far end of the Ventures signalled the start of the relay. The competitors whizzed across the tightrope and, by the time the whole team had crossed to the other side, they had incurred a time penalty point as one of them had fallen off. With Felix Road now at an advantage, we began our attempt. Although our team had made good time, two of the team had also fallen off and we lost the race due to incurring more penalties.

By mid-afternoon, a cool breeze had drifted over the Ventures and the temperature around the Olympic Village had dropped in more ways than one. Everyone appeared to be relaxed and both teams were just enjoying the day, as well as the fun of the competition. No one seemed to be so concerned about the importance of winning... except for myself and Paulette. As one of the officials, she knew the results and was aware of how close the Felix Road team was to being crowned the champions.

"You can't afford to lose any more races. You've just got to do better than St Paul's," she confided in me. Speaking over the megaphone, the official encouraged everyone to move towards the running track as quickly as they could, ready for the start of the 100 metre race. There would be one race for each age group with prizes for first, second and third places in each.

The official stood at the side of the start line and held a starting pistol in his hand. All the competitors nervously followed him, positioned themselves along the start line and waited. He said, "On your marks" and, with an outstretched arm above his head, fired once into the air. Everyone jumped, including the runners, as they took to their heels and sprinted around the course, whipping up the dust behind them.

With Guzoom in pole position, the crowd cheered and screamed, while others blew their whistles or shook and rattled their ginger beer cans, as he reached the halfway marker. His pace increased as he pulled away to cross the finish line, bringing down the ribbon as he did so. Jumping for joy, we all celebrated as he fell to the ground exhausted. The crowd surged towards him to congratulate him.

With the officials already in place for the second race, I too headed for the start line. Feeling a little apprehensive, I eyed the opposition, some of whom were much taller than myself. This was going to be a tough race, I thought.

"Focus on your own race, Cutie," Naughty Norman shouted from the crowd.

"Are you ready?" said the official. Everyone waited. "On your marks…" BANG! He fired the pistol and I began running as fast as I could. By the time we reached the halfway point, everyone was neck and neck. I heard a voice shout from the crowd, "Come on, Cutie, you can do it!" which encouraged me to keep going. With one last breath and all my strength, I lengthened my stride and accelerated to the finish line. With inches to spare, I ran through the ribbon and tripped over the finish line, crashing to the ground. With my heart beating fast and completely out of breath, I stood up unhurt to be greeted by Steve and Frank, who were on the finish line.

In unison they shouted, "You did it! You won! Well done!"

Gasping for air, I smiled and said, "Yeh."

Surrounded by the hysterical crowd, Naughty Norman and Paulette also greeted me with big smiles on their faces. She patted me on the back and handed me another bottle of water, which I was very grateful for.

"Two down and one to go," Naughty Norman shouted, clearly pleased with my efforts.

Feeling shattered, water in hand, I made my way off the track and found a pleasant spot under the shade of a chestnut tree, where I happily watched the remainder of the races. With the final two games still to go, I reflected on the day's events. I was very proud of all our achievements during the Olympics and excited knowing that I was definitely going to receive two gold medals. Overall, Felix Road would also receive even more prizes.

There was a short delay as the officials handed out the batons and coloured tabards for each team before the start of the relay race. I was excited as we had a strong team. Naughty Norman, who was captain, decided that Robert should run the first leg, Guzoom number two, Leonard number three and he would take the fourth leg.

As the teams waited at the start line, they chatted nervously about tactics until the official announced he was ready to start the race. Insisting on using the megaphone, he briefed everyone about the rules. Each person would run once around the track before handing the baton to the next person. If the baton was dropped, then that team would automatically be disqualified. With six teams in the race, there would be prizes for first, second and third positions. Knowing Naughty Norman as I did, he would only settle for first position.

Robert moved to the start line as the official announced, "Are you ready?" Holding his starting pistol, he raised his hand and said, "On your marks…" BANG.

Robert immediately took to the track, clenching the baton, and accelerated at speed towards the first marker with the other boys hot on his heels. Everyone started shouting and cheering as the gap between him and the other boys widened. With metres to spare, he crossed the line and passed the baton onto Guzoom. He too opened the gap even wider and soared around the track, leaving plumes of dust behind him. A smooth handover to Leonard and he raced up the back straight with a clear view of the finish line. Naughty Norman received the baton for the final leg of the race and, with another smooth handover, he punched through the air and accelerated at speed along the back straight, past the final marker, and headed towards the finish. Everyone was shouting and screaming as he stormed through the ribbon and crossed over the finish line. The boys ran to greet him and everyone jumped for joy as they watched the other competitors limp home in second and third place.

After a short break for the competitors to recover and refresh themselves, everyone made their way to the middle of the Olympic stadium for the final event: the tug of war. By now, several parents had arrived to watch the games and a large circle had surrounded the two teams. The official checked the rope and tied a red handkerchief in the centre of it, measuring the distance between both ends to ensure they were equal. Meanwhile, Naughty Norman gave instructions as to how our team would tackle the opposition. He was confident, having practised the tug of war in the run-up to the games, that we could win this event. He strategically placed us all along the line and reminded us to dig in deep and stand firm for as long as possible, until the opposition was pulled over the line. With butterflies in my tummy, I took up my position about halfway down the line. On the order of the official, we all reached for the rope and took up the slack. On his command, we held the rope firm until the red flag was lowered. Each side began pulling with all their might.

"Heave, heave, heave, heave!" Naughty Norman shouted as we puffed and strained while pulling on the rope.

Loud screams, cheering and rattling of ginger beer cans echoed around the Ventures, which must have been heard by all the neighbours. Everyone dug their heels deep into the ground and began pulling the opposition closer towards us. To my surprise, the other team started moving towards us. Beads of sweat trickled down my face as we struggled to keep the pressure on. I was beginning to lose my grip, as well as my balance, and the palms of my hands were becoming sweaty.

Above all the shouting, Naughty Norman shouted again, "Heave, heave, heave, heave! Come on, team, heave!"

In unison we all started to chant, "Heave! Heave! Heave!"

Little by little, we pulled the other team closer to the line. With one last effort, we pulled the front man clean over the line and he was soon followed by the rest of the team. The official dropped his flag, signalling the end of the tug of war. We all let go of the rope, causing the others to fall in a tangled heap. The other team were left deflated while everyone in our team was ecstatic. Totally exhausted, I fell to my knees gasping for air. Paulette was quickly on hand with more water, which I greedily guzzled to quench my thirst. She pointed into the crowd and there staring back at me was my mum, with the biggest smile ever on her face. I could hardly believe my eyes; she had come to watch me, even though she had told me earlier that she didn't have time for such foolishness. I smiled and waved at her before being circled by all my friends. When I looked again, she had gone.

Felix Road had come out of our Olympic Games on top and there was much need for celebrations. I was awarded three gold medals for throwing the rounders ball, the 100 metres and the tug of war. I also won a silver medal for riding the pulley. For each win, I was awarded a rosette and a packet of sweets. Not bad for an amateur, I thought.

As hosts for our Olympic Games, Steve and Frank prepared a barbecue for everyone and we celebrated well into the night. A good time was had by all.

Dad at work

Mum

Mum and Dad on their wedding day

The family. (L-R) Patsy, Mum with Veronica, Dad
(front, L-R) Keith, Elaine

Dad's mother, Ellen Douglas

Me (Cutie) and Veronica

Chapter 17

The Den

Naughty Norman was several years older than me and I regarded him as a second older brother. He lived just up the road and came from a large family of mostly boys, but he was my favourite. Like myself, he was a daily visitor to the Ventures and was well respected. He could outsmart the cleverest of boys and even the adults. He was funny and had a mischievous streak to his character, and when he spoke everyone listened and followed his antics. Besides that, he was kind and always looked out for me.

During the fruit season, Naughty Norman often went off with the older boys for an afternoon of scrumping apples from the farmer's orchard. Whenever I asked if I could tag along, he would always refuse, saying that if I got left behind or caught by the farmer wielding his shotgun who knows what would happen to me? The one time I did try to follow him, he scolded me and sent me back to the Ventures, giving me money for sweets to cheer me up. On his return, he would share his apples with me.

Naughty Norman was also a smoker and I was fascinated watching him blow smoke rings through his mouth and nostrils. He warned me that if ever he caught me smoking he would tell my brother, who would report straight back to my parents – a risk I wasn't about to take through fear of being grounded. I was also impressed by how accurately he could shoot birds in the trees with his catapult from some distance.

One day he appeared at the Ventures with a battered old moped and set about showing everyone how to ride it. He proceeded to whizz around at such speeds that no one could catch him. We placed ramps for him to ride over as he launched himself high into the air. Landing awkwardly, the back wheel would churn up a mountain of dust and he would speed off into the distance again. A couple of times he lost his balance, crashing onto the ground where he lay motionless, apparently injured. All the kids would rush to his aid and help him to his feet. A little dusty and with ripped trousers, he was up and ready to try the stunt again until he had perfected it. The older boys were allowed to have a go at performing such stunts, but none of them were as skilled as Naughty Norman. One or two fell off and actually crashed into the wall, buckling the front wheel. Nevertheless, everyone had a good time. Fun over, the moped was parked up and the older boys retreated to the far end of the Ventures where they hid away from us girls.

Paulette and I were never invited, but we followed the boys to their hideaway and, at a safe distance, positioned ourselves so that we were close enough to listen to their chatter. Naughty Norman spoke about the boys having their own space and he said that Steve had agreed for them to have a den. Steve would supervise its construction, but the boys had to make it themselves using only the materials on site. There were plenty of protests within the group, but Naughty Norman said there was a pile of wood lying around, so it was possible. Steve always kept a good supply of hammers and nails for making or repairing things, so the older boys were happy. One by one, the boys emerged from the corner and began gathering the planks of wood lying around. They glared at us, knowing that we had been eavesdropping. Naughty Norman came to our rescue.

"How much did you hear?" he asked.

"Nothing," I replied.

"Everything," Paulette answered, speaking at exactly the same time as me.

I flashed her a look of horror as she had given the game away. "We only want to help, Norm. I won't tell anyone and neither will Paulette, I promise."

"Well, you'd better not, otherwise everyone will want to use our den. I suppose you'd better make yourselves useful and help to collect some wood."

"I'm not doing that," Paulette protested as I dragged her out of earshot of the boys, who were now looking in our direction like baying wolves.

"Leave them," shouted Naughty Norman as he pushed us in the opposite direction. "Bring all the wood you can find back here."

Without another word, we were scanning the area for wood, leaving him to deal with the boys.

"Sometimes, Paulette Roberts, you need to keep your big mouth shut. We nearly got into a fight because of you."

For the first time ever, she was lost for words. Feeling satisfied that I had made my point, the moment passed and together we collected the rest of the wood. Plank by plank, Naughty Norman nailed the pieces together and in no time at all the den was finished. All that was needed to make it comfortable were a few wooden crates to use as furniture and some floor covering. A door was made with hinges and Steve provided a padlock, allowing the den to be locked when no one was around. Pleased with the finished den, Naughty Norman set off to find some more furniture, padlocking the door before he left.

"Can we go in, Norm?" we asked.

"No, not until I get back."

Paulette looked at me in dismay. She said, "I knew that was going to happen. We did all that work for nothing – I can't believe it."

She was right, of course, but I wasn't going to admit it to her. Instead, I made my way to the rabbit hutch and she followed behind me, muttering. I reached into the cage and gently pulled Snowy towards me, cradling him in my arms. Paulette continued complaining about the den. I was more concerned about the angry boys and if there would be any repercussions when Naughty Norman wasn't around, but she hadn't even given them a second thought. It had been a long day and I really didn't care about the den. Realising that I was no longer interested in her concerns, she stormed off, no doubt to complain to Steve.

Bedding Snowy down for the night, I secured the rabbit run and made my way to the gate as it was nearing closing time. Steve was impatiently waiting for everyone to leave and didn't waste any time in ushering us out of the Ventures. We watched on as he secured the gates.

"Goodnight – see you tomorrow," we said, heading down the road.

Once he was out of sight, we went back to the gate and I performed the ritual of clambering to the top and pulling Paulette over, lowering her to the other side. The Ventures was now deserted as we walked towards the den. It was still padlocked. The fire in the corner was still smouldering, though, so we added a few more logs and sat watching the glowing ashes. In no time at all, it was blazing brightly and that seemed to lighten the mood. Before long, I heard voices and immediately realised it was Naughty Norman and some of the other boys, who were sneaking back in, too. With no place to hide, we sat quietly by the fire and waited for them to arrive.

Trying to appear calm, I said, "Hello, Norm, what you doing here?"

"I should be asking you the same question. How did you get in here?"

"We climbed over," Paulette replied smugly.

He looked at the boys and they shrugged their shoulders.

"Well, I suppose you can stay then."

We smiled at each other, but neither of us said another word. Naughty Norman removed a key from his pocket and unlocked the door of the den. It was dark inside, but not for long as he produced an industrial torch from his trouser pocket and everyone laughed as he shone it into the den. The torchlight illuminated deep into the corners. It was huge inside. He smiled.

"It's my dad's torch, but he doesn't use it any more, so I borrowed it."

Placing the torch onto the floor, he turned towards the boys who were equally pleased. "Come on, guys, get the rest of the stuff."

Dutifully, the boys disappeared into the darkness, only to return a few minutes later laden with several car seats, a role of carpet and some shopping bags. Naughty Norman began laying the carpet while we all looked on. Once he'd finished, the boys handed him the car seats, which he positioned around the space. As the shopping bags were lifted into the den, the clunk of bottles could be heard. He beckoned to the boys to join him and shouts of approval could be heard. The last boy closed the door, leaving Paulette and I outside to look on. Raucous laughter echoed in our ears as they were obviously having a good time. I gestured to Paulette that we should leave them to it, but as we stood up Naughty Norman popped his head out the door.

"Where are you two going? Put some more wood on the fire," he ordered.

We did as we were told, gathering enough wood to last for a few hours and stacking it by the fire. Once finished, we again headed for the exit, but Naughty Norman called out to us.

"Come, come on inside and have some food before you go. The den belongs to you, too, as you helped to build it."

Delighted, we didn't need to be asked twice and without hesitation we crawled inside. It was amazing, so warm and cosy you could almost live in it. We finished our treats and then said that we had to go, otherwise we would get into trouble. The boys agreed and we left them to it, heading home.

No one even noticed me or what time it was when I arrived home. Everyone was too busy watching a film on TV. For a short while, I also sat and watched the film until I thought that no one had noticed my return. I quietly slipped out of the lounge and headed for my bedroom. I changed into my pyjamas, still feeling excited about the new den and how lucky we were to have been allowed inside. I told Teddy all about the day's events and he was clearly happy for me. Mum opened my bedroom door and peered around the corner.

"I touht yu was still out."

"No, Mum, I've been home for ages, but I went to the toilet and then came straight to my room."

"Oh, well, don't spen all nite talkin to dat dam Teddy."

"No, I won't, Mum. Goodnight."

"Goodnight."

She closed the door behind her. That was a close shave, I thought. I'm not going to let that happen again. Happy in my thoughts, I cuddled into Teddy, closed my eyes and fell asleep, dreaming of the den.

Stella lived around the corner from my house. She was very pretty and had long black wavy hair, which she wore in a single plait. Once she was away from home, she would let her hair hang down. She was very mature for her age, wore lots of make-up and always sported the latest fashions. She went to the same school as Keith and he often walked her home after school. He was very fond of her and they would meet at our house, where he would play the latest records in the front room.

I was allowed to listen and watch them, if I sat quietly. They practised their latest dance moves, the Bump and the Shuffle, in front of the large mirror and I would applaud them and give them scores out of ten. In between each dance, they would flop onto the sofa, laughing together when they got their moves right. Their dream was one day to perform on *Top of The Pops,* Keith said, but for now he was content in resting his head between her enormous breasts. Stella never objected and said that she loved spending time at our house. She often referred to it as a happy home full of love and affection. She loved Mum and was always sad when it was time for her to go home. Once I overheard her telling Keith that she was often beaten by her wicked stepmother and I was beginning to realise why she frequently ran away from home. She vowed to leave home when she was sixteen and never go back. This made Keith very sad, but he said that he understood.

Early one morning, Stella arrived at our house in an awful state. The buttons on her blouse had been ripped open and her hair was all matted. She was crying hysterically and shaking as she fell into Mum's arms, sobbing bitterly. She said that her stepmother had given her the beating of her life. Clutching her arms, she appeared to be in pain, which she said was caused by the buckle of a belt. Poor Stella hadn't finished her chores the previous evening and had gone to bed. When her stepmother got home from her night shift, she attacked Stella. Still sobbing and shaking, she vowed that she would never go back home and asked us to help her. But where would she live?

Mum agreed that she could stay with us until she figured things out, but then she would have to speak to Dad.

As all our parents were at work, we were able to make plans without any interruption from adults and as it was the summer holidays no one would miss Stella. She could stay at the Ventures during the day and at night, with the help of my siblings, we could sneak her into our house and keep her safe. Initially, Keith agreed, but after some thought he changed his mind.

"What if Dad comes into our room and finds Stella hiding? We will all be in for a serious beating."

I answered, "We could hide her in the den at the Ventures at night. All she has to do is climb over the gate."

"Is that what you do when you don't come home on time? I've seen you sneak through the door and run into your room, pretending that you've been there for ages."

"Well, if you tell Mum, I'll tell Dad about you and Stella," I threatened.

"Tell him what?"

I began to wish I hadn't said that as he grabbed me around the neck and forced my head towards the floor. He was hurting me, so I screamed. "I submit, I submit."

"Tell Dad what?" he demanded.

"I saw you kissing her in the front room and Dad won't like that."

Keith released his grip and sat next to me. "Alright, let's call it a truce, but if you breathe a word…"

"No, I won't. Brownie's honour."

We shook hands and remained silent for a few minutes. Stella sat in silence, too wounded to say anything.

Quietly, I said, "If you speak to Norman, he might say yes to Stella staying in the den. I know he likes her, too."

Keith flashed me another look of annoyance, stopping me in my tracks. Patsy came into the bedroom, wondering what all the commotion was about, and I told her that Keith wouldn't speak to Norman. In no time at all, my other sisters had joined us and were also threatening to tell Dad about things they knew he had done, so he would be grounded. It wasn't as if the boys weren't friends, so it made absolute sense for him to tell Naughty Norman what had happened. Backed into a corner, Keith relented and left the bedroom, closely followed by us girls. I glanced back at Stella as she lay down on the bed and pulled the sheets over her bruised body. Patsy, being the eldest girl and not afraid of Keith, opened the front door and pushed him outside, closing it swiftly behind him. We all returned to the bedroom to join Stella, but she had fallen asleep. Patsy ushered us out and we left her to rest.

A short time later, Keith returned to the house with Naughty Norman. We heard him say, "Come and see for yourself if you don't believe me. She's upstairs."

Patsy followed them towards the bedroom and opened the door. They stared at Stella. It was a pitiful sight. Not wishing to miss out on any of the drama, I squeezed myself in between the boys and sat on the bed next to Stella.

"Alright, Stella. What's going on?" asked Naughty Norman.

He entered the bedroom and Stella poured her heart out to him, showing him the weals that had appeared on her bare back.

"I told her you might let her stay in the den, Norm," I said, looking up at him hopefully.

"What did you tell her that for?"

I fell silent and lowered my head.

In chorus all my siblings, who had now joined us, said, "The den's all there is."

"But what if you get caught?" Norman asked. "Steve will take the den away from us."

It was time to reveal all. I told everyone how Paulette and I climbed into the Ventures at night and stayed there undiscovered until it was time to go home. Everyone looked at me in amazement and started to laugh. My secret was out, but I had to find a safe place for Stella. With no other alternative, Naughty Norman finally gave in and agreed to our proposed solution.

Mum had gone shopping by the time we decided to move Stella. She changed into some better clothes and left our house. We agreed to meet her at the play swings at the top of the road when the Ventures closed. In the meantime, she would visit another friend and lie low for the day. Patsy would tell Mum she had gone back home and we hoped that no further questions would be asked.

Stella would need blankets and warm clothing. Mum had a few old blankets in the back of the airing cupboard, which she no

111

longer used, and I was sure a few wouldn't be missed. Keith helped me take the bedding and some clothing to the Ventures where Naughty Norman was already waiting for us. Steve was being distracted by one of the boys, so we were able to drop off the blankets without being caught. Naughty Norman had also brought a bag of food and another industrial torch.

With everything delivered, he padlocked the den and handed Keith the key for him to pass onto Stella later. The boys left and I tried hard to act normal, waiting for Paulette to arrive. She was my closest friend, so it was only right that I let her in on our secret. She promised not to tell anyone but could not contain her excitement. To keep her from blurting out our plans, I suggested we go to the park for a change. Being away from the Ventures would also keep me distracted.

As the afternoon sun began to disappear behind the tall building across from the park, I knew that it wouldn't be long before the Ventures would close. I told Paulette I had to go home early and watched as she disappeared around the corner and out of sight. I headed back to the Ventures and nervously waited by the gate for Stella to arrive. Keith and Stella soon came running down the road, making sure they weren't being followed. Happy that the coast was clear, they watched as I confidently scaled the gate, beckoning for Stella to follow me. She began to climb up, but struggled to find her footing. Keith pushed from below, but she was far too heavy. She fell back clumsily, falling onto his head and pulling him to the ground with her. Wrapping her arms around his neck, they began to giggle.

"Come on, you two, stop messing around. Someone's going to see us and call the police."

"Well, come and help me. She's too heavy," Keith groaned.

"Well!" gasped Stella, giving Keith a stern look.

Losing my patience, I climbed back down and together we pushed her to the top of the gate, where she hung on for dear life. I clambered up behind her and, when I reached the top, helped her over to the other side. Keith followed us over, jumping down to join us on the inside of the Ventures. Stella breathed a deep sigh of relief and straightened her clothes, which had ridden up over her thighs, showing her red knickers, which amused Keith.

We made our way towards the den and she got the key from her pocket, which Keith had given her earlier, and unlocked the padlock. As the door fell open, Keith reached inside and turned on the torch. Stella gave us a big grin and crawled awkwardly into her new home. I gathered a few pieces of wood and placed them on the smouldering ashes of the fire, and in no time at all it was alight. Naughty Norman arrived, carrying a few more supplies, which Stella much appreciated. Now that she was safe, Keith said we should leave before Mum suspected anything. Stella threw her arms around us and began to weep, clearly overwhelmed with all the events of the day. We left Naughty Norman to keep her company and promised to return in the morning before the Ventures opened.

Stella remained at the Ventures undiscovered for some weeks. Eventually, her stepmother had no choice but to report her as missing to the police. The welfare department became involved and the whole sorry tale unfolded as Stella told them of her unhappy life living with her wicked stepmother. We were all ecstatic, relieved that she wasn't forced to go back home, but instead placed into a family unit where she was loved and cared for until she was old enough to find a place of her own.

Stella initially kept in touch with everyone, but after a few months she moved on. Mum often asked what happened to her on the day she had arrived at our house, but we all played ignorant, not wishing to disclose Stella's secret of sleeping in the den.

I was too young to know that I was assisting in harbouring a runaway, but Stella was my friend and I loved her very much. We had kept her safe and warm, and my only crime was to give her food and shelter.

Chapter 18

The Closure Of Felix Road
Adventure Playground

One day I arrived at the Ventures to be greeted by Steve, Frank and Christina. They seemed very quiet and not their usual selves. Gone were their happy smiles and usual banter, so my initial thoughts were that they had found out we had been hiding Stella inside the den. Other kids also noticed their glum faces. Steve then gathered us all together to announce there was going to be an important meeting, later that afternoon, with the play leaders from St Paul's and Southmead Adventure Playgrounds. All he said was that the future of the Ventures needed to be discussed. Frank handed each of us a letter and we were told to go home and fetch our parents.

I raced home, waving the piece of paper flapping in the wind, only briefly stopping to tell other kids playing in the street that they had to urgently come to the Ventures, before continuing to run up the road. Avoiding my usual ritual of swinging on the gate, I ran up to the front door, flung it open and shouted down the hallway as I entered the house. Mum was busy cooking in the kitchen.

"Mum, you have to come quick. Something's happening at the Ventures and Steve said it's urgent." I thrust the piece of paper in her direction.

She kissed her teeth and began reading the crumpled note as I stood watching, impatiently waiting for an answer.

"Lord Jesus, dem closing di Venchas," she exclaimed in her broad West Indian accent.

"We need to go now, Mum," I insisted. "Steve said everyone must come."

She set aside the vegetables she was peeling, lowered the heat under the bubbling pot of food on the cooker and followed me out of the kitchen, grabbing her coat as she marched out of the house and flung open the gate. Cursing under her breath, she buttoned up her coat, even though it wasn't cold, and headed towards Mrs Williams' house just around the corner. She banged on the door. I waited with Mum until Mrs Williams appeared, looking perplexed.

"Wot's up, Dougy?" Mrs Williams asked.

"Dem closing di Venchas. Cum mek we go see wot's goin on," Mum replied.

Without another word, both women headed down Felix Road towards the Ventures. Christina was at the gate, greeting all the visitors. I had never seen so many adults in my play space, which worried me. It was serious.

"Glad you could all come at such short notice," said Christina nervously.

"Wot di hell is dis bout? Di chile sey yu closing di Venchas. Is dat rite?" Mum asked.

"Well, we've received a letter from the council stating that they will no longer be funding several adventure playgrounds in the Bristol area. So, yes, it's true. If you carry on inside, Steve and Frank are waiting for you and will explain everything."

"But wot is dis?" Mum gasped. "Ova my ded bodi. Afta al di

work I do, fi mek mi pickney dem cum off di street."

With everyone assembled, Frank called the meeting to order. "Thank you for all coming…" he began.

"Neva mine tanks, yu meking dem tek wey di Venchas from we?" said Mrs Williams.

"Not as long as I – we – can help it. It was as much a surprise to us as it is to each and every one of you here," said Frank.

"Well, we ave fi fite fire wid fire. From I cum to dis cuntry, I bin fitin fi mi rites, an I'm not about fi giv up dis fite. Di pickney dem need dem space," Mum replied.

Frank explained that they had already been in touch with all the other adventure playgrounds in Bristol and together they were planning a protest march to lobby Bristol City Council at the Council House on College Green.

Over the next few weeks, all the kids in the area were busy making banners and painting placards for the march, which was scheduled for a weekday when all the officials and councillors would be working in their offices.

Finally, on the day of the protest, hundreds of kids were bussed in from all the other adventure playgrounds around Bristol and assembled in Portland Square, St Paul's, before we set off, waving our banners and placards, shouting at the top of our voices as we marched.

"Save our playground, save our playground!" We claimed the streets, turning right into Newfoundland Road, where a policeman had stopped the traffic as we continued our march, displaying our banners in defiance. Marching into Bond Street, we glared and shouted at passers-by, who looked on in surprise. A second policeman directed us down into The Bearpit subway, where shoppers looked on in horror as they were forced to stand aside and allow us to pass. The look of despair on some of their faces only made us shout and scream louder. The feeling of control was exhilarating.

By the time we walked into the city centre, not only was the traffic at a standstill, but workers in their offices were leaning out of their windows to see what all the fuss was about. Several loudspeakers were also encouraging us to create as much noise as possible, which we did. With our final destination only a couple of hundred yards in front of us, every child on that march was ready to fight for their respective adventure playground.

Like baying wolves, children of every cultural background stood united on the green outside the Council House, with only the ornamental fountains between us and the heart of the city's authority. Every member of staff came to their windows to look down on us as we continued noisily waving our banners. It seemed like we shouted and clapped for hours as Steve and the other play leaders made speeches and we lobbied the local member of Parliament. Oblivious as to whether he was there or not, our petition, signed by every parent, shopkeeper and child who could write, was handed to the City Council officials. I was disappointed that we were not allowed into the building, although in hindsight they were probably sensible to keep us all out. Job done and, in the hope of having achieved our objective, everyone ambled back to Portland Square. From there we were ferried back to the various adventure playgrounds.

Many months of anxious waiting went by before we heard anything from the council. Eventually, Steve and Frank came to my house and told Mum that all our efforts had paid off. The council had revoked their decision and we had won the fight to keep our cherished adventure playgrounds around the city open.

Mum was extremely proud of all our efforts. Along with other parents, they continued to support the Ventures and other community projects.

Chapter 19

Camping For The First Time

June Young was a friend of the family who had two sons, Roy and Barry. I met them through my older sisters, who often babysat for them while June went out to work. Although they were younger than me, I spent a lot of time with the boys, who became very much part of our family. Together we would go to the Ventures, where we would play for hours, and meet up with Jackie and Delroy.

June invited us all to spend the weekend camping with her and the boys. It would be my first time away from home and camping was going to be a new experience, too. I had no idea what I needed to take, but Mum as always was on hand to organise things. I watched with excitement as she packed my weekend clothes into her small vanity case with my sleeping bag strapped on top, which she forbade me to open until we had arrived at the campsite. I was so excited I could hardly contain myself and I knew that Teddy and I would have a great time.

June arrived with the boys on the Friday afternoon in her old Morris Minor Traveller, which was packed full of camping equipment.

Jackie and Delroy arrived a short time later with their parents, who chuckled as June squeezed us all into her already fully loaded car. We set off, leaving the terraced houses and smog of the city behind, arriving at Saltford in the countryside what felt like a few hours later. As the concrete footpaths disappeared, they were replaced by hedgerows on either side of the single-track road. Eventually, we came to a dirt track, drove through the open gates of a large field and parked close to the riverbank.

With the daylight fading, dusk was fast approaching and, with no time to spare, June ordered us out of the car as she unloaded everything into a heap in front of us. Under strict instructions and the supervision of Roy and Barry, who knew what they were doing, we erected both tents. It didn't take us too long as they were small. Once they were up, I wondered if we would all fit inside.

June busied herself gathering twigs and made a small fire before preparing supper. She cooked beans and sausages with bread and butter, which we all scoffed around the glow of the fire. The only other light came from the brightness of her torch as the light was fading from the sky. A cool breeze filled the air and the boys, feeling restless, wandered off to explore the hedges and riverbank while there was still some light.

In the distance, a lone fisherman was sitting quietly, holding a fishing rod. The boys approached him and they chatted for some time before returning to us with some large branches, which they had found for the fire. The man had told them that, if they were quiet, the fish would come up close to the riverbank to feed. And if he was lucky he might catch one for his supper. The boys chuckled and told him it would be much simpler to buy a piece at the fishmonger's where we lived. June laughed and explained how the fish were caught at sea and eventually ended up at the fishmonger's.

Together we sat and watched the flames of the fire as it warmed our faces, trying to process what she had said. She produced a large bag of marshmallows, saying that one day we would understand. She threaded wooden skewers through the centre of each of the marshmallows before roasting them over the fire. We all followed her lead and ate the sticky, gooey marshmallows until they were all gone and everyone felt sick from eating too many.

Still excited, the boys began play-fighting in the tent. Not wishing to get involved in their boyish antics, Jackie and I strolled along the riverbank. The sky was clear and the quietness in the countryside felt like nothing I had ever experienced. Apart from the trees rustling in the cool breeze and the ripple of the river water, no other sound could be heard. We sat cross-legged at the river's edge and listened to the beautiful sound of the night. Even the smell of the countryside was different to living in the city.

I glanced down at the glistening stream and beneath my feet saw a large fish, almost motionless in the shallows. I waved at Jackie and pointed to the fish.

She smiled back at me and said, "We didn't need a net to see a fish this big."

I smiled back at her and nodded in agreement. We watched the fish until it slowly drifted into the centre of the stream and disappeared in the deeper water. After a while, we ambled back to the tents, where June was warming some hot chocolate in a saucepan over the campfire for everyone. Eagerly, we told her what we had seen and she was delighted for us. On hearing voices, the boys bounded out of their tent and continued shoving each other.

"Listen to what the girls have been up to," June said.

"We've just seen the biggest fish by the side of the riverbank and we watched it for ages…"

Grabbing their sticks, Delroy shouted, "No way! Let's try to catch it." All three raced up the field towards the far end of the riverbank, waving their sticks high above their heads.

"…but it's gone now," continued Jackie, far too late.

We laughed as they disappeared into the darkness.

"They'll be back soon when they realise that it's gone."

Some time later, the boys returned to camp, disappointed and empty-handed. I smiled to myself and thought, if only they had listened.

June handed us a cup of hot chocolate and we all sat quietly, watching the flames in the fire while sipping our drinks. After a long day, I retreated into our small tent and rested my head on my makeshift pillow, which consisted of my favourite yellow jumper wrapped inside a towel. Happy in my new surroundings, I closed my eyes and fell into a deep sleep.

I was awoken at dawn by the sound of birdsong all around me. They were in high chorus and seemed delighted to welcome the new day. June and Jackie were still fast asleep and, not wishing to disturb them, I wriggled out of my sleeping bag, untied the strings on the tent and let myself out. The boys in the other tent were also still fast asleep, so I had a little time to explore my surroundings before breakfast.

I headed towards the riverbank and followed the sound of the birds singing in the trees above me. As they fluttered around, the overhanging branches shook loose some leaves into the awaiting water below. A couple of the birds darted overhead and swooped just above the water level, disturbing a cluster of dancing midges and breaking up the mist rising from the river. Fascinated by their display, I sat down to watch, dangling my feet in the clear water. The cool current splashed around my ankles and slowly pushed the falling leaves like small boats downstream. I couldn't quite believe what amazing sights the countryside was unfolding before my very eyes.

In the distance the sound of a church clock chimed 8am. I slowly wandered back to camp and saw June stoking the fire. It hadn't quite burnt out from the night before, so she was able to kindle the smouldering ashes. She placed a saucepan of water above it and watched it as the flames took hold. Her hair was neatly tied in a bun and she was wearing a very pretty pink dressing gown over her pyjamas. She placed six cups neatly onto a tray beside an old-fashioned metal teapot and smiled at me.

"Won't be long now. The water's nearly hot and then we can have a nice cup of tea. Did you sleep OK?"

"Oh yes, but the birds woke me up, so I went for a walk. It's lovely out here."

"Yes, I love waking up in the countryside and listening to the birds and the bees. I grew up on a farm."

"Wow, that's amazing," I said.

June described what it was like as a child, milking the cows and feeding the baby calves. She said that it was her responsibility to collect the eggs from the chickens every morning before breakfast. Then she had to cycle the two miles to the village school and back again each day.

With the water coming to the boil, she poured the hot water into the teapot and covered it with the lid. Once it had brewed, I poured myself a cup of tea and sugared it with three heaped teaspoonfuls and a drop of milk. I wondered what it would be like to live on a farm. I had never seen farm animals, apart from on the television or at a distance from inside my dad's car as they grazed in a field. I was, however, hoping that my visit to the countryside would change all that. June continued to describe how sweet the baby lambs were in the spring, together with the different smells of the farmyard. It all sounded idyllic to me in comparison to my life in the big city, which consisted of terraced houses, smelly cars and noisy engines. The only bits of greenery I saw were the small plot of land in the back garden, which had very little use, and the parks close to the Ventures.

The boys stirred and I could hear chattering and laughing coming from inside their tent. I popped my head inside, but removed it just as quickly as there was an unpleasant odour lingering in the air. Someone had blown off and the bad smell was still looming in the air. Laughter erupted from inside and I heard Roy say, "Right on cue," followed by more hysterical laughter.

June smiled. "You know what they are like – always up to no good."

I sat down beside her and finished my tea before pouring another. She opened a cool bag and produced some mushrooms, sausages, eggs, bacon, black pudding and tomatoes, and set to work with a large frying pan on the campfire. She laced the pan with a generous helping of lard and gently melted it before adding all the ingredients. In no time at all, the smell of mouthwatering cooking was wafting all around us.

Jackie peered through the flaps of the tent, looking rather dishevelled. "Mmm, that smells delicious," she said, joining us.

I handed her a cup of tea and watched her sugar it with four teaspoonfuls of sugar. June shook her head in disbelief, laughed and continued cooking breakfast.

"Isn't that tea sweet?" I asked.

"No. I used to have six, but I cut it down now."

We looked at each other and chuckled as June shook her head again. She served breakfast – what I would come to know as a 'full English' – generously smothered with tomato sauce, followed up with more tea.

After breakfast, we all walked along the riverbank, climbed over several stiles and passed cattle grazing in the fields. We were careful not to get too close and kept to the pathway. Eventually, we arrived at a beautiful riverside pub, which had once been a working mill. Alongside were a number of small boats moored up. We settled ourselves in the pub garden while June went to fetch us some drinks, watching the comings and goings of the small boats and numerous dog walkers.

With no other people of colour there, we soon drew attention to ourselves and people began staring at us. True to form, we all stared back and Jackie said, "Anyone would think that they've never seen black people before."

"Well, they need to come to Bristol."

I always felt sad when white people stared at us because they made it so obvious.

June returned with a tray of Coca-Colas and crisps for everyone and I told her that they were all staring at us.

She told us, "Pay no attention to them. It's because you are all so beautiful."

"Ain't dat di truth!" I replied.

We chatted merrily and finished our drinks before looking around the boats. Some were long and thin, and others were much higher with bigger windows and had residents on board. One nosy person even had the cheek to ask June if we were her children.

She replied, "Yes, all five of them, and aren't they darlings?"

We all laughed, waved wildly and shouted "Goodbye" before they were able to delve into our private lives any further.

After a long, exciting, adventurous day, the sun was beginning to set as we arrived back at camp. Everything seemed to be as we had left it, except for a container with a note stuck on the top. June retrieved the note, which read: 'I thought you and your friends would like to try the fish that I caught earlier today from the river. I couldn't wait any longer – enjoy. It's river trout! Yours, John. PS I'll be here tomorrow.'

"How lovely," June gasped. "Well, we don't have to worry about what's on tonight's menu now, do we?"

We all smiled, pleased that John had been so kind. He'd even gutted the fish for us.

The boys disappeared inside their tent while Jackie and I watched June light the campfire and season the fish. On a slow heat, she began cooking them over a bed of wild garlic, fresh herbs and onions. The aroma of the fish wafted through the air and my stomach juices began to come alive. I couldn't wait to tuck into our supper.

The boys reappeared as supper was almost ready and together we sat around the smouldering campfire, singing songs we had learnt from going to Scouts and Brownies, until June dished up. She had done a splendid job of ensuring the fish was cooked to perfection. It was so tender it fell off the bone. Very few words were exchanged during our delicious meal and we all tucked in ravenously. Apart from the bones, nothing was left of the delicious fish. Washing up done, we settled down to reading our books and comics until it was time for bed.

The boys made their excuses and disappeared into their tent. Jackie and I did the same, followed by June. It was proving difficult with the three of us inside, but we managed. Within a short space of time, the stench of rotten eggs wafted inside the tent. June quizzically looked at me, then Jackie, believing that one of us had blown off and started cursing. Horrified, I began to protest our innocence and quickly opened the tent flaps. By the look on our faces, she soon realised we were innocent and it was down to the boys. Muffled laughter soon erupted into loud, uncontrollable hysteria, giving the boys away. I was right that the boys had let off a stink bomb outside our tent. We spent the next few hours airing our tent to the annoyance of June. Jackie and I thought it was quite funny but concealed our amusement through fear of incurring June's wrath.

"I hope you like washing up, boys, because that's what you'll be doing tomorrow, together with collecting wood."

Feeling a little sheepish, the boys apologised and sat in silence around the fire. A cup of hot chocolate and a custard cream biscuit seemed to clear the atmosphere and soon we were all back on speaking terms. Suitably nourished, the boys washed up while we girls looked on. With another eventful day now over, we retreated into the warmth of the tent and snuggled up for the night.

On Sunday morning I was awoken again by the sounds of birdsong. June was awake and reading her book, but she wasn't aware of me staring at her. I watched as she smiled at what she was reading and snuggled under her sleeping bag, obviously enjoying her book. I didn't want to disturb her, so I feigned sleep and waited until she sat up. She glanced over in my direction and appeared startled. I giggled and sat up, too, glad that I was now able to move. She pointed to the tent flaps and we both slipped outside very quietly without disturbing Jackie.

I collected wood for the fire while June busied herself making a pot of tea. In the distance, I could see a lone figure fishing along the riverbank and wondered if it was the kind man John, who had left the fish for us the previous night. Curious, I made my way towards him and watched as he cast his hook into the stream. As I got closer, I cleared my throat and he turned towards me and smiled.

"Hello. It's a beautiful morning," he said smiling.

I nodded my head in agreement, not knowing what to say.

"Are you enjoying your holiday?" he asked.

I nodded again. What was wrong with me? I always had something to say.

"Did you get the fish I left for your supper last night?"

"Oh! Yes, it was lovely. June seasoned it up very nicely and we ate everything except the bones."

He chuckled, but I wasn't sure what he found so funny.

"We are having breakfast. Would you like a cup of tea?"

"That would be very nice, thank you." He placed his rod on the ground and the two of us set off towards the camp.

As we arrived back at the camp, I said, "This is the man who left the fish, June. I've promised him a cup of tea."

Still in her dressing gown, she became flustered and offered him a seat next to the fire. "Tea's nearly brewed. I won't be a moment – I'll just get dressed." She threw me an awkward look and disappeared inside the tent, returning a few minutes later with her hair neatly tied up in a bun and wearing a floral skirt. She looked very pretty.

Feeling a little underdressed, I excused myself and left the two adults alone.

On entering our tent, I couldn't believe that Jackie was still fast asleep. I shook her vigorously until she opened her eyes.

"What's wrong with you?" she groaned.

"Come on, you've got to get up," I whispered. "The man who brought the fish is here."

Without another word, she wriggled out of her sleeping bag, pulled on her clothes and we joined the adults. "Good morning and thanks for the fish," Jackie said to our guest.

"Oh! Hello, girls, this is John. I've invited him to stay for breakfast," June said.

"That's OK. I hope you enjoyed it?" he replied, acknowledging Jackie.

We both nodded, settled down on the ground next to him and drank our tea in silence. June continued to prepare our breakfast, which consisted of another traditional full English. As the smell wafted in the air, the boys stirred inside their tent.

"Is breakfast ready yet, Mum?" Barry shouted and June, Jackie and myself, all of us giggled.

"Come and say hello to John," she replied.

"John? John? Who's John?" asked the boys.

In no time at all, the three of them were standing outside their tent in their vests and shorts, anxious to see who John was.

"Morning lads. How you doing?"

The boys smiled and nodded. "Oh, you're the man we met the other night," said Delroy.

Introductions over, June served breakfast for everyone and we got to know a little more about John. Worried that June had forgotten the punishment she handed out to the boys for their prank the previous evening, I reminded her of it as she started clearing the breakfast dishes away.

"Oh! That's fine. Us girls can clear up while the boys go off fishing with John."

The boys chuckled and immediately disappeared into their tent, leaving me and Jackie looking on in disbelief. One after the other, they emerged and followed John towards the riverbank. I shook my head in astonishment and turned towards Jackie.

"Can you believe it? They've got away with it scot-free!"

"Oh! No, they haven't, girls. There's still work to be done. And, while they're doing that, we'll be at the pub having a glass of Coke and a packet of crisps."

"Yes!" said Jackie, punching the air as she happily cleared away the breakfast dishes.

By mid-afternoon, John had packed up and moved further down the riverbank, having not had a bite all morning. Perhaps that was because he had spent the morning with us. Or was it because the boys were making too much noise? We said our goodbyes and June admonished the boys, half in jest.

"As you haven't caught any lunch, I've had to make some sandwiches."

The boys eagerly gobbled up their lunch and were about to wander off down the riverbank again.

"Not so fast, boys. The tents need to come down and the car has to be packed before we go home. Me and the girls are going down the pub. I want it all done by the time we get back."

Jackie and I danced around, chiding the boys. They looked on in disbelief as we set off.

"But Mum!" Barry called in protest.

June merely waved her hand in the air and, without turning around, shouted, "Get on with it."

Roy punched Barry in the arm as Delroy looked on, but soon he joined in and the three boys began fighting. Although I was always happy to watch a good fight, on this occasion I was more interested in going to the pub for our drink. We arrived at the crowded pub and patiently waited at a table in the beer garden while June went inside. Drinks in tow, she emerged with John smiling, carrying crisps and peanuts for us.

"Hello, again. Where are the boys?"

"Packing," Jackie and I said in unison.

Everyone laughed and we tucked into a well-deserved treat.

We got a few stares from some of the snooty, nosy people I remembered seeing on the boats at the moorings. They obviously thought it was strange to see two white people with black kids. As young as I was, I was getting used to being stared at because of my colour.

"Ignore them," June said as I stared back. She too was used to this kind of prejudice, being the mother of two mixed-race sons.

Having had such a lovely weekend, I wasn't about to let ignorant white people spoil our fun. As we left the beer garden, I said out loud with a chuckle, "Mum, when we go home, can we have jerk chicken for tea?"

"Any ting yu want, pickney chile," she replied in her broadest Jamaican accent.

We all laughed and left the snooty people to look on in horror, leaving John to finish his beer.

The boys had done a good job of packing the car and were waiting for our return. Barry came running up to June, sporting a black eye. Roy had a cut lip and Delroy had a grazed knee. That must have been a good fight...perhaps I could ask them to re-enact it for us.

One last look at our home for the weekend and we set off through the winding single-track lanes, back to the familiar streets of the city of Bristol, which I called home.

Chapter 20

New School – New Beginnings

Mum constantly reminded me that I would be following in the footsteps of my siblings and starting at St George Lower School in the autumn, therefore homework would be my main priority. Sadly, the days of sneaking out of my house to meet Paulette at the Ventures were numbered and our rendezvous would soon come to an end.

The weekend came around and I was excited to see Paulette. I couldn't wait to tell her that Mum had received a letter from St George School confirming my place. As I scanned the Ventures, I could see her in the distance, tending to the rabbits, and quickly made my way over to join her.

"Alright, Paulette?"

"Yeh. What took you so long? I've been here for ages and the rabbits are nearly all done."

"Oh, sorry. I didn't know you were waiting for me. It's me who usually gets here first. I just get on with cleaning the rabbits until you come."

She glared at me, even though she knew I was right. She continued to stroke the rabbits.

"I've had some good news. I'm going to St George School. What school are you going to?" I asked.

"Not sure yet. I'm still waiting."

"Oh! Didn't they tell you at school?"

"Well, if they did, don't you think I would have said so?"

"Oh! Yeh." Feeling awkward, I stared at the ground in silence.

"If I don't get St George, the next school will be Whitefield and I really don't want to go there. All my friends are going to St George."

"I'm your friend, too, Paulette."

"Yes, but I've known my friends since we were at nursery."

"So, if we are going to the same school, maybe we could all be friends?"

"I don't know about that. Maybe."

Ouch! That was a blow I wasn't expecting. We had spent every day of the summer holidays together, formed a great friendship while making mischief and shared some great adventures, and there had never been any signs of her friends then. It was true that we had only become mutually acquainted through our older sisters. They thought it was a good idea for us to get to know each other since we were probably both going to the same senior school. So, I really did believe that I had become her special friend. It was me who had told her about puberty and helped her over the gates at the Ventures when it was closed. Me who had got stuck in the toilet with her and almost choked to death. I risked my life for her climbing the cherry tree, not to mention taking her down the pulley, even though she was afraid of heights. And it was me who got caught stealing the potatoes. Wasn't that real friendship?

For the first time since meeting Paulette, I wasn't so sure that she valued our friendship as much as I did. Feeling rejected, my eyes welling up, I felt it best if I leave.

"I have to go home now to try on my new school uniform, so I'll see you later."

"Alright."

Heartbroken, I turned away, wiping a tear from my eye, and left Paulette to ponder with the worry of not knowing what school she would be attending.

Taking the long way home, via the park, I slowly crunched across the broken glass and sat on the roundabout. For the first time in my young years, I felt completely alone.

With a deep sigh and one last push of the roundabout, I made my way home. As I rounded the corner, I could see Mum leaning on the gate, talking to a neighbour.

With a puzzled look on her face, she opened the gate.

"Why yu cum ome so early? Di Venchas close?"

Unable to speak, I buried my head into her apron and sobbed uncontrollably.

"Wot's wrong? Who trouble yu?"

In between sobs I blurted out, "Paulette won't be my friend at big school because she's got other friends. I only know Gary and he's a boy. He might not even be in my class, so I'm going to be all alone, Mum. I don't want to go to big school."

"Alrite, alrite, neva mine." She continued to hush me until my tears subsided. "Yu gwine fi ave a hole heap a frien. Every bodi gwine like yu. An don't yu worri bout Miss Paulette Roberts. Go lie down."

Leaving Mum chatting with the neighbour, I made my way to my bedroom, snuggled under the sheets next to Teddy and fell fast asleep.

I saw little of Paulette after that encounter as I avoided going to the Ventures. Instead, I went to the park and made new friends.

The summer nights grew shorter and the new September term was upon us. On my first day of the new term, I was up and dressed in my new school uniform by 7.30am and made my way downstairs.

Mum greeted me with a beaming smile. Reaching out towards me, she straightened the neck of my shirt and jumper, which I had opted for instead of a blazer.

"See ow nice yu look?" she said, wiping a tear from her eye before quickly turning away from me and disappearing into the kitchen.

I settled myself at the table, poured myself a cup of tea and patiently waited for my breakfast. Mum returned a few minutes later with a steaming hot bowl of porridge, which I eagerly ate. Veronica entered the dining room, still wearing her pyjamas. She slouched into the chair and yawned. I poured her a cup of tea and sugared it before handing it to her.

"Why are you up so early?" she scoffed.

"Because it's har firs day at skool an she don't wan fi be late," Mum said, handing her a bowl of porridge. "Urry up, chile."

Not wishing to start a fight, I waited patiently for her to finish.

I saw no point in making her angry until I had at least settled into my new school. After all, you never know when an older sister might come in handy.

It was 8.30am when Veronica reappeared, looking very smart in her new uniform. Mum smiled at us and handed us some pocket money. She gave Veronica strict instructions to take care of me and not to leave school without me. She then stood watching us from the front door as we set off. With butterflies dancing around in the pits of my stomach, I glanced back to see her frantically waving her white handkerchief. I waved back and walked into the path of my sister.

"Look where you're going," she scowled.

"Sorry."

"Come on, we don't want to be late on our first day."

I nodded my head in agreement, trying desperately not to cry. We continued to walk in silence as the thought of going to my new school became a reality. Veronica sensed that I was nervous and placed a reassuring arm around my shoulder.

"It's not that bad. You'll be fine. I'll meet you in the playground at break time and we can go to the tuck shop together. Alright?"

I managed a weak smile in return.

As we approached the enormous imposing building, a sickly feeling bore down heavy in the pit of my stomach again.

"I don't feel very..." and I proceeded to projectile-vomit all over my new shoes.

"That's disgusting. Come on, let's get you to the toilet and clean you up before anyone sees you like this," said my big sister, making a face.

Stepping over the pool of undigested porridge, we headed for the toilets.

Once inside, she pushed me into the corner and said, "Now listen. Listen real good, because I'm only going to say this once. Fix up yourself. Stop being so stupid. It's only a new school. Everything is going to be fine."

She promptly soaked a paper towel with cold water and smoothed it over my face. Feeling light-headed, I lowered myself onto the bench below the coat hooks and rested my head on the metal surround, the cold sensation cooling me down. With another towel, she wiped the remains of porridge from my brand new shoes.

"Who's there?" a loud voice bellowed from the corridor.

"It's Veronica Douglas, Miss. My sister wasn't feeling very well, so I'm giving her some water. She's fine now, Miss."

Veronica threw the sodden paper towels into the wastepaper bin and pulled me to my feet.

Standing in the doorway was a teacher wearing a green tracksuit.

"Hello, Miss, this is my little sister, Cute...Beverley. She was feeling a bit funny, but she's fine now. Aren't you?"

I nodded, offering a weak smile to Miss.

"I'll take her to the playground."

Without another word, Veronica dragged me out of the toilet.

We squeezed past Miss and walked down the two flights of stairs. She released my arm once we had reached the playground. Still feeling a little queasy, I gulped in the cold air, slowly breathing out again until I began to feel better. I watched in silence as Veronica greeted her friends, many of whom I knew from coming to our house or seeing them at the Ventures. After a few more deep intakes of fresh air, my head began to clear and I started to feel better. By the time the first bell of the day sounded, the feeling of nausea had vanished.

"Go on, follow them into the hall and I'll see you at break time," my sister said, pointing in the direction of the moving crowd. "You'll be fine."

I was jostled along the corridor towards the main hall with all the other first year students. A female voice shouted out instructions for everyone to hurry up and sit on the floor. It was 'Miss' who I had met earlier. Several fearsome-looking teachers stood at the front of the hall as the headmaster, Mr Long, entered. He was a well-built man, but only about five foot seven. A hushed silence filled the room as he spoke.

Moving from the playground into the hall, I had noticed the school was very diverse. However, scanning the hall, I counted only twenty black kids, no Asians in my year and the rest were white. The only person I knew from my previous school was Gary. There was also a high number of male teachers, which I had not encountered before, as the majority of the staff in my primary school had been female.

We were told that there were three separate lower school sites for the first, second and third year students. Park where I went, Rose Green and Redfield. By the time we reached the fourth and fifth year, everyone would be amalgamated into the upper school.

One by one, each teacher came forward, holding a clipboard, and began calling out the names of the students in their classes, who in turn quickly rose to their feet and stood in line.

Then 'Miss' began calling out our names.

"Beverley Douglas, Paulette Roberts, Gary Stewart…"

My heart missed a beat as I scrambled to my feet and smiled at my friends.

"I came around your house to tell you I was…" said Paulette.

"Quiet," shouted Mr Long. "No one should be talking."

Gary smiled at me, too, as we waited quietly in line.

"Right, I think that's everyone. I'm Mrs Philips, your new form tutor. Follow me, please."

The whole class shuffled out of the hall and followed Mrs Philips up two flights of stairs to our new classroom. We waited outside as she gave instructions for the seating arrangements.

"I want the first six to sit at the front, followed by the next six and so on."

The tables were positioned in rows of three that would allow two of us to sit at each table.

I immediately made my way to the front row, pulled out a chair at the far end of the row and sat down. Gary pulled out the chair beside me, followed by Paulette. It was sheer luck that we were standing behind each other when we were numbered off.

"You will remain in these seats for registration every day, so that I can remember all of your names," Mrs Philips continued, giving us instructions. She proceeded to call the register, smiling at each of us in turn, as a way of acknowledging everyone.

"Ladies, you will be pleased to know that you will all be seeing a lot more of me for English, physical education and games lessons on Friday afternoon. I do hope there are a few athletes among you."

I smiled at her, remembering how well I had performed during the Ventures Olympics.

We were reminded that the school day began at 9am sharp. If you were late, you would receive a detention. The day ended at 3.30pm. With no exception, everyone needed to be off the school grounds by then, unless you had after-school events. Mrs Philips handed everyone a folder containing a timetable detailing every lesson, the member of staff taking the lesson and the floor and number of the classroom. There was also a small purple piece of paper inside that resembled a bus ticket. She explained that the ticket was to purchase lunch, instead of using cash. At the start of the week, you would pay for your meal ticket, which would be handed out to you during registration.

This was all very confusing. I couldn't understand why we had to change classrooms after every lesson or why I needed a piece of paper to pay for my lunch.

The bell sounded again. Everyone jumped, trying to get to grips with the newness of it all. As we filed out of the classroom, Mrs Philips reminded us that the bell would sound again, signalling the end of break.

Everything appeared to be so regimented. I wondered how I would remember it all.

In single file, everyone headed for the hall.

"I'm really glad we're in the same class," I said.

"I told you it would be fine," Gary said, smiling back at me.

"Who's your friend?" asked Paulette.

"This is my friend Gary, from my old school."

"Oh," she replied.

As we were waiting in the line to purchase from the tuck shop, Veronica appeared.

"You OK?"

I nodded my head.

"What class are you in?"

"She's in the same class as me and Gary," replied Paulette.

"Oh. That's nice. I'll see you at lunchtime." Veronica squeezed my hand and smiled before she disappeared.

We purchased our snacks, found a space on the floor and sat munching away. I hadn't realised how hungry I was, having involuntarily brought up my breakfast. Still hungry, it was too late to buy anything else as the tuck shop had closed. I would just have to wait for lunch.

A group of girls approached Paulette and sat down beside her. She was extremely excited to see them. With no introductions, I guessed that they were her friends from her previous school. They chatted for a while, but she did eventually introduce me and Gary to her group of other friends.

"This is Susan, Angela, Dawn and Sandra. They are my friends from my old school."

"Hello," we all said in unison.

Unfamiliar with the art of meeting new friends or engaging in conversation, I was happy to observe the dynamics of my new peer group. Everyone chatted away, but I got the distinct impression that Paulette was in charge.

The bell sounded and everyone gathered up their belongings before we returned to our respective classrooms. As we traipsed out of the hall, we were observed by older students wearing identical badges saying 'Prefect', strategically positioned along the stairwell and corridor. "No talking, single file," echoed around us as we looked back at them.

Mrs Philips was waiting outside the classroom, still holding a hot drink in her hand. She smiled as everyone filed inside and found their seats. Closing the door behind her, she said, "As you see, there are prefects here to ensure you know where to go. They will also report any bad behaviour to your head of year, the house master or myself, so be warned."

Prefects. More like bullies, I thought. I knew I would have to watch myself around them.

The morning dragged on with more instructions about the school. I could no longer concentrate as my stomach was making loud gurgling noises, to my embarrassment and the amusement of the class. To my relief, the bell sounded as a prefect appeared at the door. We followed him to the dining hall in single file.

A life following the sound of a bell was rather daunting, but this one was a welcome reminder that it was lunchtime. I didn't have to be told twice.

The dining room was like nothing I had ever seen before. Gone was the awful smell of cabbage, as well as the dinner ladies serving behind the counter, wearing their floppy white hats and green overalls. All the food was displayed in separate counters for hot or cold, as well as a station for sandwiches and puddings. There was even the choice of fizzy drinks that you could purchase from a drinks machine.

With my dinner ticket, I paid for my lunch, then followed Paulette and Gary to a table to enjoy our food. She couldn't resist interrogating him but he was as cool as ever, not giving much away, which annoyed her. We were joined by the other girls and I continued to get to know them. Soon everyone was at ease with each other. Apart from Angela and Sandra, we all had older siblings at the school.

After lunch, we made our way back to the hall where Veronica and Kevin, Gary's older brother, were waiting for us. The girls were curious to know who they were. For the first time ever, I was proud to call her my big sister. Usually, the two of us would be fighting and bickering, but not today. She had taken care of me, made sure I arrived at school on time, cleaned me up when I was poorly and even smiled at me, which was rare, but something that I have always remembered.

By the end of the first day, I was familiar with the layout of my new school. The bell sounded for going home time. I made my way to the playground and waited for Veronica to walk me home. Together with a group of kids who also lived in Easton, we ambled home the mile and a half.

In time I became accustomed to moving around the school, together with changing classrooms for every lesson. As it turned out, Mrs Philips was only my form tutor for registration and games. When we started to follow the timetable, we were placed in classes with other kids. Apart from Susan, I ended up in the same class as my new friends.

Cookery lessons were held in Rose Green school, which meant we had to walk through the park to get there. We would leave in plenty of time, arriving well before the bell sounded. It was a double lesson that ended just before lunch. If you were still cooking by the end of the lesson, it would eat into your lunchtime. That way you would never be late for your next lesson.

In the first practical cooking lesson we were shown around the kitchen area of the classroom. It was divided into small units, each with a sink and a cooker, plus a workspace. Miss Evans began by demonstrating how to weigh out all the ingredients to make scones. Adding them into a mixing bowl, she made a dough, then cut that out in six equal portions and placed them onto a baking tray before putting them into a hot preheated oven. She set a timer and we were sent to our stations to make our own. Checking that everyone had turned on their ovens, she came around to us as we busied ourselves in the kitchen. I had no trouble following the recipe. In no time at all, I had made my scones and put them in the oven, setting the timer before closing the door.

While clearing away my workstation, I could see that my friends were also doing well in our first cookery lesson. Some of the other girls, however, seemed to be struggling with the recipe. They had flour in their hair, as well as on their faces. Miss Evans had to intervene with a couple of them, kneading their dough or adding more milk to the flour because the consistency was wrong. When everyone had placed their scones into their oven, Miss assembled the class around her again to show off her cooked scones. The aroma of baking filled the air as the scones lay cooling. They were perfect, both in colour and size. As she cut through the middle, a few crumbs fell to the side. Scooping a piece of butter from the dish, she smeared it on top of the warm scone. In seconds it found its level and melted, just as she plonked a dollop of jam on top. Cutting it in half, she bit into it, greedily munching as we looked on.

"Would anyone like to try some?" Miss asked.

We all nodded our heads, looking on as she proceeded to smother the other scones with butter and jam so that everyone could try them. They were lovely.

One by one, the timers on the ovens sounded. I returned to my workstation and grabbed a pair of oven gloves, before carefully removing the hot tray from inside. My scones were perfect. I placed them onto the cooling rack and the aroma filled the air. I was pleased with my first attempt at cooking. I stood admiring my masterpiece and listened to the gasps of joy filling the room as others took their scones out of the oven, too.

Once cooled, I put my six scones into my cake tin and waited for Miss to check that everything was tidy at the workstation. She appeared with a clipboard to inspect them.

"Very good, Beverley. You've worked well today. I am pleased with the results. I will award you ten out of ten."

I could not believe my ears. How did I manage that? She moved onto Paulette and gave her eight out of ten.

"You need to make sure you clean your workstation thoroughly, Paulette."

Paulette was not pleased. Angela scored nine points. My other friends scored ten, too. With our first cookery lesson coming to an end, we wrote down the recipe for the following week: sausage rolls. Making our way back across the park, Paulette scoffed at her marks. We all found it rather amusing. I chided her for not cleaning up properly, so she had to take it on the chin.

For the remainder of the afternoon, I had to carry my scones around with me, which was cumbersome. I also got annoyed when everyone kept asking me what was in the tin. I suppose that I would have to get used to people being interested in what I had cooked.

Veronica was excited to tell Mum I had received full marks in cooking, but I refused to let her see my scones before Mum. As soon as we arrived home, I placed the tin onto the table, lifted the lid and smiled.

Mum was chuffed to bits. "Ah! Look at dat."

"How many is there?" Veronica asked.

"Six," I replied.

"That's not enough. There's eight of us in this family. Can't you count?"

"Leave di chile alone – six is fine," Mum said.

But my sister was right. There were eight of us in the family, so someone would have to go without. I would let Mum decide on that.

The following day, Paulette had had the same dilemma. With a total of nine in her family, there were not enough scones to go around.

Mum bought extra ingredients for my next cookery class.

"Jus tell di teacha dat yu ave a big famli an ave fi cook enoff fi evry bodi."

The following week I sat in class as Miss Evans demonstrated how to make the sausage rolls. She cut them into six equal pieces and brushed them with egg yolk before placing them in the oven. How would she react when I asked her to make more? Pondering over my dilemma, I returned to my workstation and began weighing out the ingredients.

Paulette summoned Miss Evans' attention. "Miss, Beverley needs to ask you a question."

I glared at Paulette; she just couldn't help herself.

"What is it, Beverley?" Miss Evans approached my workstation and immediately saw the three-pound bag of plain flour. "That's far too much flour for six sausage rolls. Did you not read the recipe?"

"Yes, Miss, but there are eight of us in my family. My mum said that I should ask you if I could make more."

"Has anyone else got a large family?"

Except for Sandra in our group, all hands shot up.

"Well, why did no one say anything? For those with larger families, if you have enough ingredients, then double the amount."

Problem solved, I proceeded to make my sausage rolls.

At the end of the lesson, Miss awarded me with another ten out of ten. I couldn't believe it. Paulette was awarded with nine, which pleased her, too. One of the girls had burnt hers so I offered to share mine with her. Miss Evans said that it was very kind and thoughtful of me. She suggested that if everyone gave her one of theirs, we would all still have enough, so that is what we all did.

At the end of morning break, together with the girls in my class, we lined up in the main hall, waiting for our PE lesson to begin. Stacey, laden with her school bag and PE kit, decided to stop and have a chat with each of us in turn, as if she were royalty, which amused us. Throwing her bag over her shoulder, she continued to casually stroll towards the end of the line, when all of a sudden there was a loud thud, followed by an agonising groan as she crashed heavily to the ground. I turned around to see her sprawled out and giggling with embarrassment. Rubbing her arm, she slowly stood up and gathered her bag.

Unable to contain our amusement, everyone laughed hysterically at her misfortune, unaware that Mr Bennett, the sports teacher for the boys, had been watching her antics. He immediately marched over to her, just as she snuck back in line. Grabbing her by the hair, he pulled her out of the line while she protested. With everyone looking, he continued to violently drag her into his office, slamming the door behind him, leaving us all speechless. Raised voices could be heard as he shouted at Stacey aggressively, while we listened in silence. I tried to move towards the door to see if I could hear what was being said, but my feet were like lead weights and remained stuck to the ground. A choking feeling gripped my throat as I shouted, "Stop! Leave her alone!" and ran into his office, prising his large hands from her head.

In reality, no sound came out of my mouth. I was only imagining it. Instead, I stared hopelessly at the battered, wooden door, realising there was nothing I could do to stop her pain. Anger and sadness bubbled up inside me as we waited for it all to stop. Involuntary tears welled up in my eyes and slowly trickled down my face. A deep-rooted wave of rage suddenly filled my head and my heartbeat quickened, while the insides of my stomach tensed, forcing me to catch my breath. Clenching my fists, I dug my nails deep into my sweaty palms, because I suddenly remembered the horror of my first day at infant school all those years ago. I was desperately trying to push back the disturbing image of that poor lad being beaten by Mrs Price. Unfortunately, no amount of discomfort could take away those miserable thoughts and erase the memories of that fateful day. The sadness of more than five years ago came flooding back into the forefront of my mind and I was witnessing the horror of abuse all over again.

Stacey came out of the office a short time later with her head lowered, cradling her arm across her chest. With matted hair, a red face and silent tears streaming down her face, she stood back in line, snivelling.

Posturing in front of us, Mr Bennett followed her, then walked the full length of the line, glaring at each one of us in turn. As he stood in front of me, our eyes met. Warm tears still staining my cheeks, I wanted him to see that he had caused me pain, too, and I refused to avoid looking at him. I was deeply upset and angry that he had assaulted a girl. I also felt ashamed that I was too scared to help my friend. He was a bully, as well as a coward. I had lost all respect for him and would never forget what he did.

Everyone remained in silence as the sound of footsteps entered the hall. Mrs Philips had finally arrived to take the class. As she approached, Mr Bennett immediately ushered her into the office, closing the door behind him. My only thought was that he was concocting lies to cover his arse. However, the whole class had witnessed his brutal assault and, should anyone ever ask me, I wouldn't hold back on telling the truth.

Mrs Philips came out of the office looking flushed and muttering under her breath, as she ushered us into the changing room. Traumatised,

I dried my eyes and contemplated what I should do next. Mrs Philips barked instructions at us to get changed while she took Stacey to one side. She excused Stacey from the lesson, telling us that she wasn't feeling well. That was the last we saw of her that day. I later learned that she had gone home. After that incident, I vowed that no one would ever put their hands on me without feeling the wrath of me or my parents. By the time we had reached the third year of school, Mr Bennett had left.

That kind of bullying, abusive behaviour, or any other corporal punishment, would not be tolerated or accepted today.

Stacey and I became close friends after that day, but we never spoke of that incident. A shy girl with a big heart and a great sense of humour, she often came to school covered in bruises, which she said were from being thrown off her horse because he decided to stop short of a jump. However, it never deterred her and she would dust herself off before climbing back into the saddle again. It all seemed exciting and a far cry from how I spent my leisure time. We agreed that one day I would meet her horse.

Her love of horses was evident when she produced some amazing sketches of them during art lessons. When she was bored in class, she would make sketches in the back of her exercise books. If ever she was caught, she would simply flip the pages over so that the teacher was none the wiser.

Eventually, I did meet Stacey's horse, Marquis, and she showed me how to groom and lunge him (which is when you exercise a horse by holding a long line attached to them as they move around you in a circle). She also taught me how to ride him and, as an adult, I continued to ride for many years.

After leaving school, we went our separate ways. It wasn't until we were in our forties that we met up again through a mutual friend. Her love for animals continues and she still keeps horses.

At eleven, I won my first cross-country race during a games lesson. After that, Mrs Philips entered me into other races. I represented the school and competed in numerous competitions. I was an all-rounder in sports – a keen athlete, netball and rounders player. I also captained both teams.

At fourteen, I went to the upper school where those of us who had been split between the different lower schools were joined together. I met up with Paulette again, who had moved to Redfield Lower School, because it was much closer to her home. Not having seen her for a year meant our friendship had changed, and we had both made new friends. I was spending more time with Stacey and our lunchtimes were spent in the local café or outside Clarkes pie shop. Most of the girls I mixed with smoked. It was not long before I tried it, too. At break time everyone squeezed into a single cubicle of the toilets for a quick puff. There was always someone looking out, so no one ever got caught. The staff knew what we were up to, but turned a blind eye.

The options for games also changed, so you could go ice skating at the ice rink next to the Top Rank nightclub in the centre of Bristol. I borrowed a pair of boots from a friend until I managed to buy a pair of second-hand Bauer hockey boots of my own. When I left school, I continued ice skating for several years afterwards.

This love of sport continued into my adulthood and, by the time I joined the Special Constabulary, not only was I fit, but I also joined the netball team, competing with other forces and the police volleyball team.

During Mr Harris' maths lesson, Stacey and I sat next to each other. Whenever he had his back to us while writing on the board, we would chatter among ourselves. Without warning, he would turn around and hurl a piece of chalk across the room at us. Once he caught Stacey in the centre of her chest. Those who didn't have their heads buried in their books followed its flight. They all stared at us as I stifled a laugh. Mr Harris picked up another piece of chalk and continued writing on the board as though nothing had happened. Once he finished, he casually said, "You see, sometimes chalk has a mind of its own."

During another lesson, he threw the board rubber across the room. It landed in the middle of our desk, creating plumes of chalk dust around us. That silenced us.

One day, Yvonne came home with some jacks. They were metal star-shaped figures that you could buy in a packet of five. You also needed a small ball for the game. The idea was that you threw the jacks onto the floor, threw the ball into the air, allowed it to bounce once, scooped up a single jack and then caught the ball. Once you had all the jacks, you would throw them onto the floor and collect two, the object being to pick up all the jacks in one scoop before moving onto the second round. This became a popular pastime every day that kept everyone occupied before school, at break times and during the lunch break.

Chapter 21

Christmas

Christmas in our house was an exciting time. Mum always ordered a massive turkey that barely fit in the small oven. Along with the turkey, we had all the trimmings and vegetables as well as our traditional rice and peas for the big day. We also had a Christmas hamper, a treat that was not to be opened until Boxing Day. It was filled with our favourite foods, tins of ham, chocolates, biscuits, tinned fruit, sherry, dates and much, much more. Mum would place it in the front room and give strict instructions not to touch it. Dad would also bring home bottles of spirits and a special bottle of Mum's favourite drink Advocaat, Babycham or Pony.

Each year the four-foot artificial Christmas tree, together with all the stars, holly and plastic baubles, would be taken from the attic and the decorations would lovingly be placed around the house. The tree, dressed in all its flashing lights, tinsel and glitter, would take its pride of place in the front room, in the centre of the bay window on top of the glass cabinet. From the outside, it looked as though it was six feet tall; in reality it was nearly half that size. When any of my friends came to visit they were sworn to secrecy never to divulge the true size of our tree. A few presents would be placed under it, which made the front room feel Christmassy. Dad would also dust off his special collection of records – The Rat Pack, Tom Jones and Jim Reeves, together with his Jamaican reggae and calypso music – all ready to entertain any visitors over the festive period.

On Christmas Eve, Dad would go off to the pub and we would stay at home with Mum and help prepare the turkey, vegetables and all the lovely food for Christmas Day. With eight mouths to feed there was a lot to prepare, so we would all be busy peeling, chopping and making stuffing. Being around Mum while she had the odd glass of sherry made it fun, too. She quickly became tipsy and would have to lie down, leaving us to finish preparing the vegetables…and the remainder of her sherry. When everything was done, we would all sit around the television and enjoy the evening's entertainment.

Back then, most families couldn't afford expensive gifts. Nevertheless, it didn't stop us getting excited about Christmas morning and wondering what Father Christmas was going to bring us. A doll or perhaps a few games would be nice, so before I went to bed I would remind him that I had been good – well, for some of the time at least – and I deserved something special. After all, what kid did you know who was good all of the time? Which made me believe that I had to be in with a chance.

In their own way, Mum and Dad made sure everything was more than special. They gave us love and affection, and ensured we never missed out. It was more important being around all the family and enjoying a good feast over Christmas than anything we were given.

Friends would visit during the holiday period and I would listen to them telling stories about the good old days before they came to England. Christmas in the Caribbean was completely different from the wintry Christmas in Britain. They talked of outings where they would spend the whole day catching fish with the local fishermen in St Ann's Bay, near Ocho Rios. They were taught how to clean and gut their catch. Once back on shore, they would make a fire before wrapping the fish inside banana leaves, then roasting them over the smoking fire. When cooked, they would share the food and use their fingers to eat the succulent fish. They loved attending the church picnic where they could spend hours playing cricket on the sandy beaches. All the young men would try to impress the pastor's daughter or other local girls, but no one ever succeeded.

The men shared stories of their youth 'back home' while growing up in Jamaica. Many lived in the countryside where most of the work was on the land. They talked of the hours they spent after school cutting sugar cane in the fields and having to wait by the roadside for it to be collected. They would amuse themselves by climbing the coconut trees, throwing half-eaten mangos at the barking dogs and flirting with the young girls walking by, hoping that one might notice them, but always aware that they might be under the watchful glare of their mothers. Dad said you knew a girl was interested if she smiled and looked back at you. They spoke of drinking rum and getting high smoking ganja at all-night parties in someone's 'yard'. Everyone laughed hysterically as Dad retold a story of one of his friends passing out at such a party because he was stoned...they watched him as he slowly slid down the wall and ended up snoring on the ground. Then, as the dawn broke, Dad said they left the friend where he had fallen and went home without him.

Dad also remembered his own father buying a piglet to be fattened up throughout the year, ready for slaughter before Christmas. There were no butchers' shops in the countryside back then, so the slaughterman took the pig to his premises and, under the supervision of the government official, it would be killed, cut up and signed off. My granddad would then distribute the portions of meat around the family and sell some of the meat around the village, sometimes happy to receive a bottle of rum in payment.

Years later, when I finally visited Jamaica, I also experienced for myself some of those amazing goings-on when I visited Dad's sister, my late aunt, in Spanish Town. She had her own land, which was plentiful in orange, lemon, grapefruit, banana and mango trees. There were ackee, cocoa and coffee trees, too, none of which I had ever seen before. With an abundance of vegetables such as yams, plantain, callaloo and Scotch bonnet peppers, she was self-sufficient. There were also chickens and a huge pig, which she proudly told me she had reared from a small piglet and fattened up for the Christmas table. I never had the joy of spending Christmas with my aunt, but having been a guest at her dinner table, I knew that she would have put on a magnificent feast for Christmas.

Back at home, Christmas morning was different. I was woken up by the smell of bacon wafting under my nose. Instantly, I knew Dad was cooking breakfast. Pushing Teddy aside, I ran downstairs and into the kitchen. As predicted, Dad was waiting for my arrival. He glanced up from the stove where a large frying pan was sizzling away on the hob filled with eggs, bacon, mushrooms and fried bread.

I smiled at him and said, "Alright, Daddy."

"Alrite fi yu," he replied, then handed me a warm plate and continued to serve me my breakfast.

"Thanks, Daddy. Merry Christmas."

He grunted something, but I was too engrossed in my plate full of food as I sat at the table and got stuck into my full English breakfast. One by one, my sisters and brother joined me and Dad handed them their breakfast, too. I cleared my plate and positioned myself on the sofa, turned on the television and became engulfed in the magic of Christmas Day.

Mum came down later that morning and started busying herself with cooking Christmas dinner. She was a little subdued, but the scarf tied around her head was an indication that she had a headache, probably from drinking too much sherry the night before. Dad gave her a mischievous squeeze and patted her on the behind before slipping out of the kitchen.

"Soon cum," was all he said as he pulled on his heavy coat and disappeared out the door.

In Jamaican, the term 'soon cum' is as long or short a time as you wish; there is no expectation of time. We all knew that he was off to the pub to join his friends and would return sometime later after the pub had closed. Usually that would be just before dinner was about to be served. There were times when he didn't quite make dinner and Mum would be furious. She would send Keith to the pub to get him, giving strict instructions that he should not leave without him. Dad would return holding on to my brother's arm, trying to pretend he was sober. Knowing that Mum was annoyed with him, he would sit quietly until dinner was served.

The living room would be rearranged with the dining table extended to fit everyone around it. Mum and Dad would sit at either end with everyone else to the side of them. This was the only day that we would all sit together without any squabbles. Mum would place the turkey in front of Dad to carve and he would pull off a leg and take a bite out of it before starting to carve the large succulent bird. This annoyed Mum, who insisted that we say a prayer of thanksgiving before the feast would begin. Dinner would be followed by a traditional Christmas pudding or trifle, after which we would all lounge about on the sofa, waiting for the Queen's speech to start. By the time she began, Dad would be fast asleep and snoring in his chair.

Thankful for my presents, which consisted of a dolly, snakes and ladders and a few items of clothing, I was happy that Father Christmas had delivered. Perhaps next year I might even ask for a bicycle.

Chapter 22

Youth Clubs

The Mill Youth Club was within walking distance of our house. It was run by youth leaders Mr Lynch, Tim and Wendy. As a popular safe place where friends from school or kids from the local area could meet up, it was always well attended by teenagers from Easton, as well as St Paul's. The club comprised a purpose-built sports hall, complete with a trampoline, and a separate television room, plus a large communal space used for table tennis and table football. There was a small bar area where you could purchase soft drinks or snacks, but only the adults were allowed behind the bar. Outside there was a tennis court, which was marked out for football, plus a netball court.

Yvonne was about fourteen when she and Sharon, Paulette's older sister, started going to the club. That was when they became part of the netball team, Seven Steppers, which was run by Wendy. Whenever they played a home game, everyone came out to support them. They were a good team for such a young side.

I was about twelve when Paulette and I started going to the club and mixing with the older kids. Many of them were underage smokers, which was still fashionable despite growing awareness of the health implications. However, the staff turned a blind eye as they were more interested in watching television or gossiping behind the bar. I realised later that those areas were a good vantage point from which the staff could see everything that was going on, including the area just outside the reception. The only place that was not overlooked from the bar was the television room; that's probably why Tim spent so much time in there. Hence, we were always under the watchful eye of someone on the staff without it being obvious.

One evening I saw Yvonne and Sharon disappearing around the side of the building, so I decided to follow them. Partially hidden behind a couple of waste bins, the two were huddled in a corner and plumes of smoke wafted above their heads. They were smoking and I couldn't contain my shock.

"What are you doing?" I knew very well what they were doing. I marched up to them as they desperately tried to hide their cigarettes.

"What does it look like?" Yvonne said.

"You're going to be in big trouble when I tell Daddy."

"Go on then, but if you do it's no more going to trampolining or club for you," she replied.

"Why's that?" I asked.

"You won't be able to come here on your own, so go ahead, tell Daddy."

I thought about it for a few moments.

"Alright then. I won't say anything."

Disgusted, without another word, I left them to finish their cigarettes.

Once a week, in the early evening, I attended trampolining sessions, which Wendy organised for anyone who was interested in gymnastics. I enjoyed the thrill of jumping in the air, catapulting into star jumps and learning how to do backward flips. Afterwards I would go into the club where I would wait for Yvonne to join me. At that time the club was quiet, so I could select my favourite records on the jukebox, then play table football or table tennis with the younger kids until the older boys arrived. Leaving them to it, I would meet up with my sister, Sharon and Paulette.

Every month the older boys would set up their sound system (for records) and blast out the latest reggae tunes on vinyl forty-fives for everybody to enjoy. I would stand around the edge of the dance floor, watching everyone, before copying their moves. There was always lots of laughter around when someone introduced a new dance. When the lights lowered, the tempo of the music would also change to the lovers' rock, a slow dance. The boys would grab a girl by the hand and lead her into a dark corner. In very close quarters, together they would smooch in time to the music. Unfortunately for the young lovers, Mr Lynch was never too far away to put a stop to anything too daring, to the annoyance of the courting couple. The lights would be turned up and the music would change again to a more upbeat rhythm. Gradually, the dancing would come to an end as everyone was ushered out of the club. If we were too slow departing, Mr Lynch unbuckled his belt from around his waist, folded it in two and began threatening everyone with a beating. He didn't have to tell me twice; I was the first one out of the door. Loitering in the car park, I could see kids laughing and screaming as they ran towards me, followed by Mr Lynch thrashing his belt around like a mad man. Everyone made their way towards the road, heckling at him with shouts of "Bald head, Mr Lynch, you're too old to catch us!"

We all knew that he was a well-respected member of the community, known to all our parents. So, it was no use going home to complain because you would end up getting a cursing for not listening to him.

I make Mr Lynch sound like he was an ogre, but he was dealing with some pretty rebellious teenagers. In fact, he was very kind and caring. He was a role model and mentor to many. He also organised several trips for the older kids, as well as helping them to find employment. They often told stories of getting licks with his strap, but it was all in good humour.

Yvonne and I often walked with Sharon to see her home after leaving the club if she was there on her own. It was never any bother since she didn't live too far from our house, so even with this little detour we would still be home in plenty of time before Mum would start worrying about us. Our parents always reminded us that there was safety in numbers, so on the occasion that we were late we had a good enough excuse.

I remember it being a chilly winter's evening; a full moon lit up the night sky and there were hardly any people about. There also seemed to be fewer cars on the road, which gave me an eerie feeling inside, so I was reluctant to walk Sharon home. However, Yvonne wouldn't allow me to walk home by myself, so we stayed together. After what seemed ages, we walked along the dual carriageway and I was pleased to see Lawrence Hill roundabout come into view. This was as far as we needed to go with Sharon before we, too, could make our own way home.

Standing close to the metal railings as we stood talking for a few minutes, I noticed a blue transit van with large white lettering on the side, which read 'Securicor', drive past us. As it did so, the brake lights flashed on and it stopped. Then I heard the sound of its brakes screech as the van reversed at speed back towards us. Before it stopped, the passenger door flew open and then I heard the alarming sound of rattling chains. A large figure wearing dark overalls and a helmet leapt out of the van and started running towards us.

Yvonne immediately grabbed my arm and shouted, "Run!"

Sheer fright and adrenalin carried me as I ran as fast as my legs would take me towards Sharon's house, which luckily was only a few hundred yards away. She lived on a small estate so we were able to lose ourselves in among the alleyways only known to the local residents. As luck would have it, her neighbour was standing in his driveway as we ran past him.

"What's the rush?" he shouted.

"A man with chains is chasing us," we shouted, continuing to run.

I was petrified as my heart pounded heavily against my chest. Sharon and Yvonne were only a few feet ahead of me, but it seemed like a mile and I was terrified. Fearing that I would be left behind and caught, I began to scream and cry hysterically. "Yvonne, don't leave me," I begged.

She immediately slowed down and I was able to catch up as they both stopped running. Fearing we were still being chased, I continued running until I had reached Sharon's front garden. Panic-stricken and shaking, I fell to my knees exhausted, buried my head in my hands and sobbed.

I heard a male voice shout. "There's no one following you. It's alright."

Sharon and Yvonne stood by her gate, breathing heavily and gasping for air.

"Cutie, where are you?" asked Yvonne.

Terrified, I cried even louder, unable to speak but hoping she would hear me.

"Come." Coaxing me from my hiding place, she opened the gate and pulled me towards her and I cried some more.

"Hush, hush. It's gonna be alright."

Sharon's neighbour, who I recognised as Renick, joined us. "What's wrong? What happened to you?"

Sharon began to tell him what had happened and I cried some more. Yvonne tried to console me, but I was inconsolable. How would we get home safely? Sharon suggested we remain at her house until things died down, but Mum would be worrying. Yvonne said that if Mum found out we had been chased by someone who she thought was the National Front, we certainly wouldn't be allowed out for the evenings that followed.

Renick agreed and volunteered to walk us home. Before we set off, he returned to his house and emerged holding a large kitchen knife. "This is my mum's best knife, so I need to bring it back."

I was now even more worried and unsure why he needed a knife.

Smiling back at me, he said, "Don't worry. It's for our protection."

As he concealed it up his sleeve, we bade Sharon goodnight, promising to see her the following day, and set off home with Renick as our knight in shining armour.

Either side of Renick, Yvonne and I nervously held on tight to his arms. As we left the estate, we changed our route home, following Trinity Road into Stapleton Road. Every time the illuminated headlights of a vehicle travelled towards us, panic took hold of me and I began to tremble until it had gone past, then I relaxed again. With The Lebeq pub in sight, we were nearly home. Arriving at the bottom of our road, I hugged Renick, thanking him for seeing us home safely.

Yvonne took hold of my cold, trembling hand and rubbed it gently before she asked, "You alright?"

I nodded my head, still confused and frightened after our horrendous ordeal.

"Let's not tell Mummy or Daddy just yet. I'll find a time to tell them tomorrow, so don't say anything, otherwise we won't be able to go out again."

My sister had a point, so I agreed to keep our little secret from my parents.

The next day Yvonne was in Keith's bedroom. The door was slightly ajar and I could see them sitting on the bed next to each other. She was telling him what had happened to us the previous evening. By the look on his face, he was none too pleased. I knocked tentatively on the door and waited to be invited in. Looking round the door, he saw that it was me. He simply said, "Come."

On entering, I squeezed my small frame in between them and sat quietly as they carried on talking. Keith put his arm around me and gave me a comforting hug. I listened quietly to my older siblings as they talked about other incidents involving a group called the National Front. Keith said that this was typical behaviour of this racist organisation.

I was confused. This kind of talk scared me and I started to cry. Comforted by my sister and brother, we agreed that we would tell Mr Lynch at the club before speaking with our parents. Keith said that it would be better coming from him because there were other racist attacks happening to black people in the area. So, that was how things were left.

As time went on, I spent less time staying out late, preferring to come home before the youth club ended. Being chased and scared out of my wits had left me mentally scarred. Sharon got a lift home after the club, so she didn't have to walk home alone late at night either. I remember my parents were extremely cautious about allowing us to be out too late in the evenings, unless we were in groups or accompanied by an adult. Mum spoke to all of us about what had happened, but I was too traumatised at the time to relive it and soon I tried to forget about it.

Years later, I realised that we had walked past Trinity Road Police Station on that fateful day. Perhaps we should have reported the incident. However, had Renick been searched by the police, he would have been arrested for carrying an offensive weapon, even though he was only trying to protect us from being attacked.

I also understood how big the National Front movement had grown and how dangerous it was. I cannot say for certain that it was them who chased us on that dreadful night, but the question still looms to this day. Why would men driving around in a Securicor security van scare the living daylights out of three kids, brandishing chains? It still scares me to think what would have happened if he had caught up with us. Suffice to say that I remained vigilant as a young girl living in and around Bristol in the 1970s.

As Yvonne and Veronica got older, they began to frequent the Docklands Settlement Youth Club in St Paul's. Like The Mill Youth Club, it was well attended by many black kids who lived in the area. It provided a safe, social, community hub, where you were able to escape, communicate in your own language and enjoy reggae music. With our parents leaving Jamaica in the 50s, young people found it difficult to connect with their cultural roots in the UK. They had to deal with being constantly stopped and searched, being harassed by the police, and racially abused, which in turn caused resentment towards authority. These youth clubs were the only cultural connection or link to Jamaica where, through music, we could relate together, as first-generation immigrants born in Britain. Indoor activities of table tennis, martial arts and five-a-side football were also a welcome distraction for youngsters. The highlight of being at the club was to be able to enjoy listening to the rival DJs playing the latest reggae music imported from Jamaica. Massive hand-crafted speaker boxes, almost the size of wardrobes, were placed at either end of the room, and the sound of heavy bass music blasted out for everyone to enjoy. This space continues to provide a special meeting place for young people in the community.

My sisters also went to dances we called 'the blues' on the weekend, sneaking out late at night after Dad had returned home from the pub. They became involved in the Rastafarian movement, let their hair grow into locks and became vegetarians.

On the rare occasion I went with them, Yvonne would wrap my hair in a head wrap (turban). We would turn up at a house where the blues was happening, walk down the basement steps and knock on the front door. A pair of eyes would peer through a makeshift opening behind a red light. The bolt made a memorable sound as it slid across the door for us to gain entry. With the distinct smell of weed and the heavy bass sounds of reggae music blasting out, in total darkness we would feel our way around the room. After a few minutes, my eyes would adjust, but still I could only vaguely make out the silhouette of people standing around. One of the only forms of light would come from the momentary flame of a lighter or matchstick, which was usually long enough for you to be able to recognise people's faces. The other light came from the DJ stand in the corner of the room. It was annoying when he would rewind a record two or three times before allowing it to play to the end, to the delight of the crowd. Alcoholic drinks in a plastic cup or a plate of curry goat, served from the makeshift kitchen, could be bought. A plate of food always satisfied my hunger. No one ever left the blues until daylight, so you would often hear the hum of a milk float and the clatter of bottles as the milkman did his rounds.

Veronica was also heavily involved with the West Indian dance team that toured around the south of England, which meant I didn't spend much time with her. Being close in age, we squabbled a lot, so I kept my distance.

My first under-eighteens disco was at a nightclub called Dreamland where they played soul or funky music all night. Everyone wore their best disco outfits to match the huge glitter balls in the centre of the dance floor. From the minute the music started, it was customary for everyone to crowd onto the dance floor to show off their latest moves. If you were any good, everyone would gravitate towards you. Just as you were getting into the rhythm of the beat, the records would cut in for the slow dance, stopping everyone except the couples dead in their tracks. After a few slow tunes, the DJ would play the same familiar tune that signalled the end of the night. By 11.30pm the lights would go up and everyone would starburst into the corners, wiping beads of sweat from their brow, before peeling off in groups to make their way home.

Chapter 23

St John Ambulance

I joined St John Ambulance in 1977, at the age of thirteen. We were known as Bristol Number One Nursing and Cadet Division, situated at the headquarters in Woodborough Street. It has since been demolished and replaced with private homes. The object of the cadet division was to learn and practise First Aid, as well as Home Nursing, to promote health and gain life skills. Sally, a larger-than-life woman, oversaw the running of the division, which had a diverse membership of young girls eager to learn. Sally had a big heart, was passionate about her work and cared very deeply about the principles of First Aid. In fact, many of the cadets she taught went on to fulfil careers in nursing.

After a few months of regular attendance, paying my subs each week as well as showing commitment, I was given a grey uniform with a black beret, which I wore with pride. I soon gained many skills and certificates of proficiency in First Aid and Home Nursing. My friends Susan, Angela and Dawn joined a year later. In time they, too, became proficient enough to be awarded certificates for their efforts.

Every year there was an annual divisional inspection attended by the commandant and superintendent for the area. As they entered the room, we would be called to attention and they would inspect us, stopping briefly for a chat.

Like the Brownies, St John Ambulance had their own pledge, the Cadet Code of Chivalry, which we recited at the end of every meeting. We promised to be loyal to the Queen and to our officers, to do everything well to help those in need, to be kind to all animals and to be happy and truthful in everything that we did.

At sixteen I was made Cadet of the Year and the following year I won first prize in a competition for a poster I made. By 1983, I was heavily involved in my voluntary work. In the December of that year, I was chosen to be a flagbearer at the St Mary Redcliffe Church Christmas ceremony. I was also immensely proud to have been selected to read the Third Lesson, which was from St John Chapter 1, verses 18–25.

For one week in the year, we would go around door to door making collections. Not only was it a positive way of meeting or helping the community, but we were also successful in actively recruiting new cadets. While out collecting, Sally was particularly good at assessing people's needs. She would contact Help the Aged, the doctor's surgery or the community nurse to ensure they were given support. After a First Aid class, I would accompany a senior member to the home of a local resident to check on their welfare. In many cases, a half-hour visit or a chat over a cup of tea made a huge difference to their lives. My time was recognised as duty hours and would go towards recognition for the work I did in the community.

My skills as a First Aider were put into action for the first time after witnessing a road traffic accident. I was collecting money for the charity Christmas carol bus, which used to drive around the streets of

Bristol, when a cyclist collided with a car. He was conscious, but had dislocated his shoulder. I immediately tended to him by wrapping my scarf around his arm to keep it in place until I was able to place it into a sling, making him more comfortable. Once the ambulance arrived, he was taken to hospital. Sally was pleased to hear how swiftly I had reacted to the situation.

As an adult member, one of my more envied tasks was First Aid duties at the Bristol Hippodrome, the main theatre in the city, with Sonia, who was also an adult member and a few years older than me. She was also responsible for teaching the younger cadets. Dressed in our uniforms and with our First Aid kit bags, we would arrive at the Hippodrome, make our way to the back of the stalls and be on standby in case someone in the audience needed our help. Fortunately, no one ever became unwell on my watch, which was great as I loved watching live theatre performances – especially as they were all free. I also became involved in competitions with Sally and Sonia, but that didn't last long. I always forgot what signs I needed to look for in a patient to gain any points. However, Sally and Sonia made up for my shortcomings and always got full marks for their efforts.

Having taken and failed the entrance exam for the army at the age of sixteen, not only was I extremely disappointed, but I was also at a complete loss as to what career path I should take. As much as I loved doing my First Aid, I didn't want to become a nurse. My only option was to attend college. While studying, I remained a member of St John Ambulance and it was by sheer accident that one of our lecturers, Ken, joined our division. One day he arrived in his police uniform. Everyone was so interested in what he did that the lesson was taken up with numerous questions regarding the police. He showed us his handcuffs, whistle and wooden truncheon, along with sharing stories of life on the beat. It all sounded extremely exciting. After every lecture I would make a beeline for him and quiz him some more about his antics in the police. One day, he asked me if I would be interested in becoming a police officer. I really hadn't given a career in the police any thought. However, having planted the seed, I began thinking about it seriously.

Ken must have told Sally that I had shown an interest in the police. She encouraged me to leave my options open and handed me an information pack about the Special Constabulary, which Ken had left for me. Although the opportunities were different from the army, being a special constable meant that I could still live at home, it was voluntary and I could choose the hours I worked. In the small print, it also said that I could go on to become a regular police constable. That would mean becoming full-time and being paid, something I would later consider.

Chapter 24

College

On leaving school at fifteen, I started a course in community care at Brunel College. By the end of the second term, I was bored and began bunking off lessons. I managed to get through the first year, but my heart wasn't in it so I decided to leave. Having only attained four CSE qualifications at school, the job market was not looking promising for me. I made the decision to change course and study for my O-levels.

At Soundwell College, there was a huge difference in attitudes between the tutors and students. I was treated like an adult and, in addition, both my English and maths teachers gave me a lot of encouragement to learn. I saw my first production of *Romeo and Juliet* at The Old Vic theatre, which I loved. I studied hard, gaining three of my four qualifications within the two years I was there. I also made some new friends, Juliet, Sherrie and Jennifer, with whom I have continued to remain friends.

My new friends introduced me to the adult club scene. With a full face of make-up and high heels, together with a pretty smile, we all passed as being over eighteen, gaining entry to enjoy such clubs as The Dug Out and Romeo and Juliets. I also discovered booze and the opposite sex.

Jennifer had left home by the time we finished our second year at college, which planted the seed for me to think about finding somewhere of my own. When I broached the subject with Mum, she wasn't happy. I guess, as I was the youngest and the last to leave home, she worried that little bit more. However, things came to a head following an argument after my eighteenth birthday, so I left home. Initially, I stayed with my sister Elaine, who had her own flat, before I found a bedsit of my own.

After leaving college, I got a job working in an old people's home, but it was poorly paid so to make ends meet I found a second job working in a bar. With tips I could just about manage to pay the rent, however, the excitement of living on my own soon wore off. Being skint was no fun. Neither was living on beans and toast. For the first year, I couldn't afford to go out socially, which left me feeling lonely and isolated.

My break came when I was offered a seasonal job at Cadbury chocolate factory in Keynsham, where I got a temporary role. Veronica was also working there, which was a bonus and we ended up working there for a couple of years. Dad took us to and from work, which saved on travel costs. Although it was shift work, it paid extremely well. Then, after being made redundant, I began working for the employment service or dole office. I also continued going to evening classes to gain a few more O-levels.

It was at this time I became acquainted with Avon and Somerset Constabulary, and in 1983 I became a special constable.

Chapter 25

A Good Day Turns Bad

Wednesday 19 November 1986. I was twenty-two and living in my own flat, not far from my parents. The alarm clock sounded and woke me from a deep sleep. Slowly reaching for the off button, I hit snooze, shutting out the dulcet tones of the radio presenter and snuggling back under the warmth of my duvet. Just as I was drifting off again, the melodies of Marvin Gaye filled the silence.

With a heavy sigh, I reluctantly threw back the duvet, sat on the edge of the bed and lazily stumbled to my feet. With the room still in darkness, I carefully felt my way along the furniture and into the bathroom next door. Reaching for the light switch, I squinted my eyes in preparation for the momentary blindness from the bright fluorescent light that invaded my consciousness. As my pupils adjusted, I stared into the mirror, sighed again and pulled faces at the reflection staring back at me. Wearily, I turned on the cold tap and braced myself for the shock that followed as I splashed my face with cold water to remove the sleep from my eyes. Running my damp fingers through my thick, natty hair, which had taken on its own ruffled style, I groomed myself back into the present. Returning to my bedroom, I got dressed and ran downstairs into the kitchen. I am not a morning person!

Two cups of tea and a slice of toast later, I was ready for the day that lay ahead and set off for work. By now I was employed as a civil servant working in the benefits office in the centre of Bristol. Initially my job seemed very glamorous, but in reality it was simply a case of 'signing on' clients who were unemployed, processing their information into the telex machine and sending it to central office.

The highlight of my job was visiting the satellite offices around the region, where we would set up shop for the claimants who lived in rural areas. It was a long day, but it meant that I could build up flexitime to later take off as I saw fit.

I was particularly interested in the clients who were fraudulently working and claiming benefits, and I made it my business to refer them to the supervisor. She in turn would pass the file onto the fraud squad, who would gather the evidence and, where necessary, prosecute them. My referrals were rarely wrong and it paid off when I landed a job with the regional fraud office. I was able to assist with investigations out in the field, gathering vital evidence to secure a prosecution. I developed my investigative skills and prepared case files, which was to prove invaluable in my future career as a police officer.

It was around mid-morning when my manager summoned me to her office. Feeling a little anxious, I sat down in the chair, racking my brain for something I had done. Instead, she took great delight in telling me that a referral I had submitted had snowballed into a cross-border investigation of illegal workers. There were several arrests and several 'clients' had been prosecuted. For my good work, I was rewarded with a ten-pound voucher.

I left the office feeling pleased with myself and couldn't wait to share the good news with my mum. When I rang her later, she was very pleased for me and said I deserved a celebratory meal. We agreed that I would go home after work when I could fill her in with the details. My manager shared my success with my colleagues, treating us all to cream cakes. With the end of another productive working day, I said goodbye to the girls in my office and headed home.

I loved going home to my parents' house as it was filled with unconditional love and happiness. Home was my safe haven and every visit felt as if time had stood still in the Douglas household.

Looking back, I have very fond memories of running out of school at the end of the day and rushing home to be with my mum. She would wait patiently, leaning on the iron gate in the front garden, which was in desperate need of oiling. Dad refused to oil it as he said he could hear when someone came to the house.

Mum would be pleasantly rattling on to everyone who walked by and keeping an eye out for us, her children, as we appeared one by one at the top of the road. The happiness on her face when she saw me gave me the best feeling in the world, knowing she had missed me and I her. Knowing that I was always famished after a hard day at school, she would fling open the gate and welcome me home. I would head straight inside and to the kitchen, where a hot meal waited for me on a low heat in the oven.

I loved her so much that whenever I saved up enough pocket money I would surprise her with a quarter-pound of fudge or a fresh cream slice, which were her favourite treats, and she always made a big fuss to show her appreciation.

During dinner, Mum would sit opposite me while I eagerly scoffed her delicious cooking and the conversation always began with her asking me, "Wot did yu do at skool toda?"

"Not much. Just played a bit."

"An wot did yu ave fi dinna?"

Well, that question was always easy. I always knew the answer to that. "Meat and vegetables and a pudding with custard."

"Well, ow cum yu so ungri if yu eat so much food?"

"Because they don't cook like you, Mum, and they don't know how to make the food taste good."

She would chuckle and smile sweetly at me before disappearing into the kitchen.

Today, however, there was no sign of Mum waiting to greet me at the gate. If it was too cold outside, she would peer through the window from behind the curtains in the front room and smile at me as I walked down the path. Perhaps today, she was busy in the kitchen. I pushed open the front door, which was always on the latch, and entered the hallway. I was greeted by the familiar smells of her delicious home cooking, so I expected she was in the kitchen. Strangely, the house was very quiet.

I shouted out, but there was no reply and an eerie feeling came over me as I slowly opened the lounge door. A plume of white smoke hung in the air from a freshly lit cigarette... Dad was home. How unusual, I thought.

He was sitting quietly at the dining room table, sipping a cup of tea. He nodded and carried on pulling hard on his cigarette. Patsy was also in the room, looking very worried, but neither of them said a word. I glanced over to the sofa where I saw Mum lying motionless with her eyes closed. I presumed she was suffering from one of her headaches. Not realising then that she was unwell, I headed into the kitchen to see what was for dinner. While helping myself from the big pot of food, Patsy joined me.

"Mum's not well."

Without hesitation I re-entered the lounge, sat on the sofa beside Mum and looked into her eyes. No smile, no conversation – instead, a vacant hollow look staring back at me. I thought she had had another nervous breakdown, only this time she was unable to speak and I didn't know why. Gently, I placed my hand on her forehead and stroked her softly.

"It's alright, Mummy. I'm here now with Daddy and Patsy."

She didn't respond. Her breathing was very shallow and I voiced my concerns to Dad. Looking very worried, he nodded in agreement, said the doctor was on his way and continued to sip his tea. Silence filled the room once more. Patsy and I decided to make Mum look presentable before the doctor arrived. As a very proud woman, we knew she would be cross if he saw her in her house clothes.

Together, we eventually managed to get her to stand before walking her the short distance along the hallway to her bedroom on the ground floor. There was something very wrong and she was unable to stand unaided. Her arms were very limp and, as we walked her along the narrow hallway, I noticed her foot dragging lazily along the floor behind her. On reaching the bedroom, we gently lowered her down onto the bed where she lay conscious but motionless. We changed her clothes in preparation for the doctor's arrival, placed her under the sheets and waited for him to arrive.

Before long, there was a knock on the front door and I could hear Dad rushing along the hallway to greet the doctor. After a short conversation, both men entered the bedroom. We were ushered out and the door was abruptly closed behind us. We sat on the steps outside and waited in silence for what seemed like hours. The long wait made me feel sick in the pit of my stomach. My heart was pounding and all I wanted to do was burst into tears. Suddenly the door opened and my heart began to beat even louder in my chest. Biting down hard on the insides of my cheeks, yet unaware of the pain, I stared at my dad. He ushered us back into the lounge, saying only that Mum would be going to hospital. Leaving us with worrying thoughts, he returned to the bedroom and closed the door behind him.

The doctor emerged from the bedroom looking very grim. I went in and saw that Mum was still lying very still, in the same position we had left her in earlier. Her nightdress and the bedclothes were ruffled, so I knew that the doctor had examined her. I began to straighten her nightdress and, as I did so, Mum briefly opened her eyes. She looked very confused and tried to speak to me, but she only managed to move her lower jaw and no sound came out.

"It's OK, Mummy, you don't need to say anything."

I smiled back at her as tears filled both our eyes and I knew this was not good. Gently kissing her clammy cheek, I smoothed my hand across her forehead before climbing onto the bed and laying next to her, caressing her warm body next to mine.

A loud and impatient knock on the front door startled me. Peering through the crack in the door, I could see Dad and the doctor as they emerged from the front room and the doctor opened the front door. Two ambulance men stood outside, holding large bags. In lowered voices the doctor briefly spoke with them before they all came into the bedroom. I was ushered out again and the door was closed firmly behind me. After another long wait and feeling utterly helpless, I thought perhaps this would be a good time for me to pray. Clasping my hands tightly together, I closed my eyes. Trying hard not to cry, I calmed my breath, breathing in and out very slowly, which helped to slow down my heartbeat. "Dear God, please..."

The door swiftly opened and one of the ambulance men emerged out of the bedroom and headed towards the front door.

"What's happening?" I asked.

He didn't reply and gave me a weak smile as he reached the rear of the ambulance, opened the door and removed a stretcher from inside. My heart sank as he awkwardly wheeled it into the house and disappeared back into the bedroom, closing the door behind him. The front door was slightly ajar and I could see a small crowd loitering outside the house. I prayed for them to go away. I prayed, too, that God would watch over my mother and keep her safe. The bedroom door opened again and Mum, lying on the stretcher, was wheeled out of the house. As the crowd looked on, I could hear voices saying, "Poor Mrs Douglas."

Safely inside the privacy of the ambulance, the doctor told us that Mum was very poorly and had suffered a stroke. She needed to be in hospital and he promised to look after her. I didn't know how seriously ill Mum was, but I was sure she would be well again in only a matter of weeks. Dad travelled to the hospital with her and left us behind to tell the rest of the family what had happened. This was going to be a long and emotional night, and no one knew how it would end.

A Turn For The Worse

Dad didn't return home until after midnight. He was exhausted and in no fit state to be quizzed; neither did I have the energy for small talk. We sat in silence for what seemed like an age before I sighed and began gathering up my things. I waited patiently by the door until he looked up at me. Slowly, he removed a cigarette from its box, tapped it on the outside, ignited his Zipper lighter and pulled back hard, filling his lungs with smoke. He momentarily held his breath before exhaling a plume of white smoke, which filled the room. This seemed to relax him and the worry lines on his brow appeared to soften.

"Di docta dem lookin afta Mammi. Dem will no more tomorra. She's sleepin now an dares notink fi worri bout. She's in di bes place."

"That's good, Dad," I said, trying to sound positive and feeling optimistic that we would know more in the morning. "I'll be off then."

"It's too late fi yu fi walk ome now. Why don't yu stop ere tonite?"

For once, I was happy to accept his invitation. I kissed him on the cheek and made my way to my old bedroom. Exhausted, I wearily climbed up the stairs and entered my old room, which was now the spare room for when grandchildren came to stay. Apart from a few toys and toddlers' clothes, not much had changed. Immediately, all my happy childhood memories and the security of living at home came rushing back.

I had left home at eighteen and made a pact with myself never to live at home again. Thinking that I was a big woman back then, Miss Independent, I wanted to show everyone I could make it on my own. But tonight I was happy to be home and, at twenty-two, albeit under difficult circumstances, I was in no hurry to leave. Wearily, I lowered myself onto my old single bed and lay my head on the pillow. I smiled to myself as I remembered telling Mum I was dying, when in fact I had started my period. And the day she caught me, Rapunzel, swooshing her golden hair around while wearing my favourite yellow jumper attached to my head. Pinching the potatoes to take down to the Ventures and getting caught by Dad. It was all too much for me and I began to cry uncontrollably. Burying my head deep into the softness of my pillow, I prayed that Dad couldn't hear me.

I'm not sure how long I cried for, but I was awoken the following morning by the sound of birdsong coming from the garden. I snuggled back under the sheets, happy to be in my old room, and then I remembered why I had returned home. Mum had taken ill and had spent the night in hospital.

With a heavy heart, I pulled myself out of bed and went into the bathroom. I felt like crap and I looked even worse. My eyes were bloodshot and swollen, a clear indication of how much I had been crying. Not wishing to alarm Dad, I bathed my eyes in cold water until the swelling had gone down and I looked a little more presentable. As I descended the stairs, I could hear voices coming from the lounge, but I needn't have worried as it was only the morning television presenters keeping Dad company. He was sitting at the table, with a cigarette smouldering away in the ashtray, and sipping a cup of tea. I wondered if he had been there all night.

"Morning, Dad."

He glanced up with a weak smile.

"Yu wan a cup a tea, Spallydew?"

I smiled back and sat in the chair next to him. Lost in the moment, I treasured him using my nickname, something he hadn't done since I was a child. Before I could answer, he began pouring me a cup, which he had set aside for me. Or was it for Mum? Grateful, I slurped my tea and we watched the news in silence.

Chapter 26

Thursday 20 November 1986

Dad was anxious to return to the hospital, so by the time I had finished my tea he was heading out the door. "Soon cum. Mi call yu afta mi speak to di docta."

In anticipation of my siblings and other well-wishers visiting, I reluctantly remained behind and retreated to the warmth of the lounge, poured myself another cup of tea and continued watching television. One by one, my siblings trickled through the door, each of them anxious for an update. Dad had given me strict instructions for us to wait until he had seen Mum and spoken to the doctor before we could visit. This upset everyone and arguments overshadowed Dad's wishes, which was certainly not what either of my parents would have wanted under the circumstances. The atmosphere was beginning to stifle me and I felt under pressure as everyone wanted to take control. Dad needed to be in control of the situation and he really couldn't cope with the emotions of his children. Surely, they could understand that?

To avoid any further arguments, I headed for the garden. Leaning back against the wall, I closed my eyes and allowed the crisp winter breeze to brush over my face. I remembered collecting the eggs from the small chicken coop Dad had built, which was now his tool shed. I loved planting daffodils – Mum's favourite flowers – in pots and watching them grow in the spring, as well as picking the runner beans and sharing them with the neighbours. A small garden, but very productive.

The familiar soft touch of the cat's bushy tail brushing against my legs disturbed my thoughts. Our family cat was a seventeen-year-old dirty, fat, old moggy that had lost many of his teeth due to Dad feeding him chicken bones.

"Oh, Charlie Boy, we forgot all about you."

Leaning down, I picked him up, cradled him in my arms and stroked his head. He purred back at me in appreciation for the attention. "Age getting the better of you, old boy?"

With all that had gone on in the last twenty-four hours, no one had remembered to feed Charlie Boy and he was not going to let another day go by. He leapt out of my arms and ran into the kitchen, with me following. He sat patiently beside his bowl and started meowing at me. I smiled and reached into the cupboard to find his favourite food. At the sound of the tin being opened, he impatiently began loudly purring and paced around my legs as I emptied the contents into his bowl. As soon as I had placed it on the floor, he got stuck in. Giving him a final stroke on his back, I left him to enjoy his food.

With the heated voices of my siblings still coming from the lounge, I decided it best to avoid any further confrontation. I yanked open the lounge door and, before anyone could say anything to me, I headed for the door on the other side of the room, made my excuses and returned to my bedroom. Filled with despair, I lay on my bed and stared vacantly at the ceiling, closed my eyes and eventually drifted off. I was awoken by the sound of the phone ringing. Throwing back the bedclothes, I ran downstairs and flung open the lounge door. Nervously I stared at the receiver, not wanting to answer it, but I knew it had to be news about Mum.

"Hello."

"It's Daddi."

"Any news?" I asked anxiously.

"Mammi's ad a good nite, but dares no change. Dem teking har fi a brain scan so dats gwine tek all day. Dares no point unu cumin to di ospital til lata."

Without uttering another word, I handed the phone over to Patsy. While my other siblings gathered around her, I moved to the back of the room as I saw the opportunity to take myself off for a walk. I had no idea where my legs would take me, but I just followed my heart.

Turning left out of the gate that still screeched and needed oiling, I walked past the junction of Felix Road and paused for a moment as a childhood memory popped into my mind. Here, every Sunday afternoon, the ice-cream man would park his van and repeatedly play that familiar tune on a loop until the children ran out to greet him. We would form an orderly queue and wait patiently to be served. He called all the girls Cynthia and all the boys Winston, even though none of us had those names. Mum always had an ice cream with a chocolate flake, smothered with nuts and strawberry syrup. I was allowed to have a cider ice lolly.

Continuing along St Gabriel's Road, I stopped briefly outside Hemmings Wasters, the forbidden gates that gave access only to the large dumper trucks. Continuing to Bouverie Street, I remembered St Gabriel's Church with the school attached to it, although long gone now and replaced by housing. Around the corner a little further on was The Pit Pony pub, where Dad sometimes drank and played darts. If ever I saw his car in the car park, I would make it my business to rattle on the off-licence window and summon him outside. After my first visit, he knew it was me and would come outside holding seven packets of crisps for me, Mum and my siblings. The Pit Pony pub had seen better days even then and was now boarded up.

Further ahead, on the opposite side of the road, I could see the familiar multicoloured swings in the park. The gravelled area, where many of us local kids had received cuts and grazes, had also been modernised and replaced with rubber for health and safety reasons. The park was no longer littered with shards of broken glass, but very well maintained. I pushed a swing to and fro before squeezing my large frame into the rubber seat and began rocking backwards and forwards until I reached an exhilarating height. With the wind in my hair, I felt as free as a bird, as if I hadn't a care in the world.

As the swing slowed down, I glanced across the park to the other side of the road. As young girls, Paulette and I would climb onto the roof of the electricity generating house and talk for hours without ever being discovered. The swing came to a halt and I wriggled out of it and stared across the park. Instinctively, I walked across the grass towards the top end of Felix Road, where the adventure playground stood: the Ventures. The gates, which I had clambered over daily, had been replaced and, as I walked the short distance towards them, a feeling of joy rushed over me. I peered inside, remembering the world of my childhood happiness and all the memories I'd left behind still locked inside me. Now fully renovated and modern, the clubhouse had been built to an extremely high standard. The pulley, the basketball court and all the wooden playing structures were still in the same place but updated. As for the den, that had long gone. Overwhelmed with countless emotions, I knew that I had truly come home again. With renewed vigour and a sense of calm, I was able to return to the house.

Dad arrived home early that evening and told us we could visit Mum. Excited, we donned coats and set off to the hospital, arriving there as the ward staff were clearing away the dishes from the evening meal.

As I approached Mum's bed, no dirty dishes were in sight. Instead, she was lying on her back, apparently resting. A nurse joined us and said she hadn't regained consciousness, but they were hopeful that she would. A crushing pain grabbed my heart as I held Mum's hand open, kissing it before pressing it against my cheek. She didn't respond. I looked at Dad, but his eyes fell to the floor, where they remained until the chatter of my siblings became too loud and he snapped at them to lower their voices. Three hours later, the nurse entered the cubicle and said visiting time had ended over an hour ago and we were asked to leave.

I kissed Mum and whispered, "I love you, Mummy," before leaving her side. We drove home in silence and, once inside the house, I remembered where Dad kept his secret stash of Jamaican Wray and Nephew white rum. Without asking him, I entered his bedroom, removed the bottle from inside his wardrobe and tucked it under my arm. I helped myself to the best glasses from the glass cabinet in the front room and joined him in the lounge. Setting down the glasses in front of him, I promptly filled our glasses and chased the rum with a splash of Coke. He nodded and raised his glass. Without a word, I headed towards the kitchen and removed the ice tray from the fridge. Mum was probably the last person to refill the ice tray, I thought. Feeling overwhelmed, I twisted the tray, releasing the ice cubes into a bowl, and returned to the lounge. Raising our glasses, we sipped our drinks, contemplating the moment, and I was able to compose myself a bit.

Reflecting on the day's events, I was pleased that I had spent some time with Mum, but I was still extremely concerned about her condition. Tonight wasn't the right time to ask too many questions. It could wait for another day, so I made my excuses and went to bed.

Snuggled under the sheets, my thoughts drifted back to my earlier visit to the adventure playground. Peering through the gates had ignited precious memories I had locked away in the back of my mind. Feeling warm inside, I was soon fast asleep.

Chapter 27

Friday 21 November 1986

I was woken up by the smell of bacon drifting up the stairs and it reminded me of the days when Dad would cook breakfast on the weekend. I knew it was going to be a feast of a fry-up he had concocted using the previous day's leftovers. As well as eggs, bacon, beans, sausages and plantains with fried bread, it was served with hot cups of tea, made with Ideal milk (evaporated milk in a tin), which would set me up for the day. Coming to, I scrambled out of bed, raced downstairs and pushed open the lounge door, to be greeted by Dad with a big smile on his face.

"Mi no it wudn't tek yu long."

I smiled back at him and sat at the table as he promptly poured me a cup of tea. Today there were six mugs set on the table, which indicated that we had guests or he was expecting visitors.

I wasn't aware that anyone else was in the house, but my siblings must have arrived after I had gone to bed the previous night. One by one, they emerged from the other bedrooms and we all sat at the table and enjoyed Dad's hearty fry-up. After breakfast, Dad made a few phone calls to our relatives in Derby, giving them an update on Mum's progress. My younger nieces and nephews also came to visit to find out how Mum was. The house very quickly filled with laughter, just like old times, which helped to lighten the underlying tension of her absence. Preparations were made to pack a bag for her, which Dad would take to the hospital later that day, when we all hoped to learn more about her condition.

Mid-morning, Dad left for the hospital and promised to update us as soon as he had spoken to the doctor. Within an hour, the phone rang.

"Hello."

"It's Daddi. Mammi's still avin tests, but yu can cum to di ospital dis evenin."

"How is she, Dad?" I asked.

"Oh, yu no, alrite."

I wasn't convinced, but he wouldn't say any more and with that he ended the call. Not wishing to raise the alarm, I told my siblings that Mum was fine and would be having more tests; after that, the doctors would know more. Before they could bombard me with questions, I said, "Soon cum," and I left them to it.

When I returned to the house a few hours later, Dad was home, too. The family had left, except for Veronica, who was busy in the kitchen cooking dinner. The delicious smell of herbs and spices wafted throughout the house, making me feel hungry. She was the best cook of all us girls and, like Mum, she put her love and affection into every meal she made. It wasn't long before she had prepared a big pot of Caribbean cuisine, which she left simmering on the cooker for everyone – for when Dad was ready to eat or for anyone else who cared to visit. Once I was sure she had left the house, I helped myself to a small plate of food to tide me over. It was delicious and I couldn't wait for dinner time to come when I could eat until my belly was full.

Early that evening, the phone rang and I overheard the person on the other end of the line ask Dad to go to the hospital. We drove there together in silence. When we arrived, the ward sister met us and, ushering us into her office, explained that there was no change in Mum's condition. A brain scan confirmed she'd had a massive stroke and we should prepare ourselves for the worst. In stunned silence and disbelief, I left her office and headed straight towards Mum's bed, where the curtains were drawn around her. She was covered with a thin white cotton sheet. Her nightdress, which she had been wearing the day before, had been removed and replaced with a hospital gown, which was thrown across her body. Her eyes were closed and she appeared to be in a deep sleep.

"Hello, Mummy, it's me, Cutie."

Leaning forward, I kissed her warm cheek and took her hand into mine. She didn't stir. I sat in the chair next to her and silently watched her chest rise and fall with every shallow breath she took. My eyes filled with tears and I forced a smile, feeling helpless, knowing that there was nothing I could do. Hearing voices outside, I quickly wiped away my tears. Dad and the doctor entered the cubicle and stood either side of my mum.

"We've carried out eighteen different brain scans on Mrs Douglas and, unfortunately, the left side of her brain is very severely damaged. She hasn't regained consciousness since being admitted to the ward and neither has she showed any signs of change."

"Will she get betta?" Dad asked.

The doctor, slowly shaking his head, looked first at me and then at Dad.

"I'm afraid I can't really say. It's been more than twenty-four hours and her condition hasn't changed. It depends if she regains consciousness. At the moment, Mr Douglas, your wife hasn't showed any signs of improvement, so all we can do is wait."

A massive pain surged through my chest and I fell backwards into the chair. I couldn't believe what I was hearing.

"How long?" Dad asked.

"She's stable now and we'll keep monitoring her. Perhaps this is a good time to ask your family to come in to see your wife."

"Is my mum going to die?"

"Let's see how she is in the morning."

He lowered his gaze. Tears filled my eyes and I cried hysterically, but there was no sound. My whole life was shattered and I was heartbroken. The doctor didn't answer my question, but I knew by the expression on his face he didn't hold much hope.

"What shall we do, Daddy?"

Shocked and in silence, we both looked at Mum. She looked so peaceful. After a while, clearing his throat and drying his eyes, Dad broke the silence.

"Well, we ave fi tell evry bodi. Yu tink Mammi will be alrite til we cum bac?"

"She's stable now, but every minute is precious." The doctor left us alone.

I hugged and kissed Mum, reassuring her that we would be back with my siblings very soon and reluctantly we left the ward. We made our way home to inform the family, returning to the hospital an hour or so later. Mum was still unconscious and hadn't changed her position. Everyone rallied around her, trying to make light of the sadness of the moment. With six of us around her bed, the nurse let us into the small cubicle, for which we were grateful. We took it in turns smoothing over the sheets while waiting for Mum to stir or open her eyes, but it wasn't to be. Hours later, the nurse peered around the curtain to inform us that visiting time was over. The time had gone so quickly and it was difficult to leave. Would this be our last visit or the last time that I would see my mum alive? No one knew.

Dad held open the curtain as we quietly filed out of the cubicle and he stayed behind. The nurse nodded at him and told us that he might be a while, persuading us to leave him behind. I have no idea of how I got home that evening or much about the days that followed, as one seemed to roll into another.

I returned to my flat, which had stood empty for a while, and realised how empty my life had become. It was stiflingly hot inside the hallway as I had forgotten to turn off the heating. The only sound I could hear was coming from the dripping tap inside the kitchen. As I pushed the door open, I remembered leaving the sink full of dirty dishes and mould had started growing inside the teacups I had left on the side. The rubbish bin, which I had also forgotten to empty, was smelling of rotting food and the heat only made it worse.

I opened the balcony door, releasing the stench, and stepped outside into my virtual roof garden. Living on the fourteenth floor of a high-rise apartment had its benefits, one being that the flat had spectacular views of the city and beyond, which was second to none. With no one to disturb me, I created my own stories about what was happening around me. Here I could also put the world to rights without being challenged by anyone, but nothing would change the fate of my mum's future. With a heavy heart, I cleaned the kitchen and gathered some clean clothes before heading back to Dad's house.

By the time I arrived, Dad was waiting for me. We made our way back to the hospital ward where the nurse was waiting for us. She ushered us into her office, closing the door behind her. She sat in her chair and shifted awkwardly as she spoke. There was sadness in her eyes.

"I'm so sorry to have to tell you, Mr Douglas. Mrs Douglas slipped away peacefully just after you left."

In disbelief I made my way to her bedside and slipped through the curtains where she lay very still, as if sleeping. Heartbroken and overwhelmed with grief, I cried uncontrollably and slid my hand gently over her silky warm body. She couldn't have been gone long. Why wasn't I with her? I placed my head on her chest and said, "Sorry, Mummy."

A soft voice behind me spoke. "No, child, she wasn't alone. I was with her until the end."

I collapsed into the comfort of the nurse's arms as she clasped me close to her, holding my shaking body as I sobbed. Dad came into the cubicle and held Mum's hand. I turned to thank the nurse, but she had disappeared.

"Where is the nurse?"

"It's jus yu, me and yu mudda ere, no bodi else."

I couldn't explain what had happened to me, but I believe it was Mum's guardian angel comforting me, so perhaps she was not alone after all. One last look and I said my final goodbye to the woman I called my mother; my idol, my love, my happiness all gone forever.

Chapter 28

Making Plans

The sudden death of my mother left me with an incredible sense of loss, unimaginable pain that cut into the deepest parts of my soul. I was left completely heartbroken and felt insufferable emptiness, which affected me for many years, even after laying her to rest. Her death came without any warning, like an uninvited guest, and took her from me. All I have now are the memories of a wonderful woman who always put things right and made me the woman I am today.

Word soon got around of Mum's passing. In the true Caribbean tradition, Dad began receiving family and friends into our home. He busied himself arranging her funeral and final send-off, which included the Nine-Nights period of mourning that would last for seven days and seven nights. With all that he had to arrange, there was no time for him to start his own grieving process. Clearly a broken man, without making a fuss, he began organising everything. I was of little comfort to him as I couldn't deal with my own emotions. Neither could I face returning to my empty flat, nor being on my own for any length of time. I suppose I was scared, so I stayed on at the house. Friends and neighbours dropped by to share in our grief and stayed with us for hours and hours, singing hymns, playing dominoes, drinking and eating lots, so we all had to play host to our grieving friends. My sleep became more erratic as my head fought with the guilt of the last forty-eight hours. I was still trying to process the fact that Mum was dead, and that she had died alone.

When some of Dad's friends had left, I was able to retreat to the comfort and security of my old bedroom. Here I found the solace that I needed when things got too much for me. I was also able to block out some of the pain with a few large rums each night before I went to sleep. With each day running into the next, I was never sure exactly what day it was.

The tradition of the Nine-Nights for some families has changed in the UK, as it is a costly expense. Now families tend to have one night of celebrating the deceased prior to the funeral and wake.

I woke up one morning in bed with a thumping headache. I sat up and the room began to spin. A watery sensation filled my mouth and a sickly feeling swirled around in my stomach. Unable to move, I violently vomited the contents of my stomach all over the bedclothes. With snot and mostly alcohol seeping through my nostrils, the stench of rum from the night before lingered in the air.

Involuntary tears rolled down my cheeks and my head pounded as I struggled to roll the bedding up into a bundle and carried everything into the bathroom, dropping it into the bath. As I turned the cold tap over the sheets, I could feel the contents of my stomach bubbling up towards my mouth again. Changing my position slightly, I leaned over the toilet, dropped to my knees, retched and vomited again. Hugging the rim of the toilet with one hand, I grabbed the toilet paper beside me. Pulling a generous amount off, I blew my nose and small deposits of food wedged between my throat and nasal passage dislodged into the soft tissue. Rolling the used tissue into a ball,

I dropped it down the pan and pulled the flush. Still on my knees, I crawled towards the bath, turned off the running water and removed the bedding from inside. It was much heavier now that the sheets were wet, but I managed to shake the vomit into the toilet. The smell was overwhelming and I vomited again.

Hugging the toilet as if it were my best friend, I remained on the floor until the pain in my head eased and I was able to return the dirty sheets to soak. A few deep breaths and my stomach started churning again. I scrambled back towards the toilet and hugged the rim as I vomited the last traces of bile from my stomach. With the sheets soaking, I washed my face, headed back to my bedroom and collapsed onto the bed, closing my eyes. I felt awful and my only wish was to crawl back into bed and shut out the world. I was in no fit state to see anyone who cared to visit the family.

Lying in bed reduced the throbbing in my head and I thought it best to stay in this position until the pain had disappeared. There was a knock on the door and Dad appeared, holding a cup of tea. He placed it on the side table and smiled at me.

"Look like yu need fi stay ina yu bed chile."

"I don't feel very well, Dad."

"Mi tell yu fi slow down on di rum. It's not fi di weak-arted, yu no."

"I know, Dad."

My eyes followed him as he turned away and headed for the door, closing it quietly behind him, and I was left to nurse my hangover. I could hear voices coming from downstairs, none of whom I recognised. The clock on the bedside table displayed 9.30am and Dad hadn't had much sleep. I wanted to help, but I was too poorly to meet anyone. Whoever it was, Dad was telling them of the sad events that led to Mum being admitted to hospital and of her passing away. Unable to control their shock and disbelief, there were cries of, "Oh no! Oh God! Poor Mrs Douglas! I can't believe it."

Dad must have ushered them into the lounge as their voices became more muffled. No doubt he would make them a sweet, hot cup of tea to help them deal with the shock. Broken-hearted, I buried my head into the pillow and sobbed myself to sleep.

Chapter 29

The Laying Out Of My Mother

I entered the undertakers' carpentry workshop which was at the rear of the Chapel of Rest and in the next room, there she was. Quite still, ice-cold, but looking unbelievably beautiful. Her hair glistened under the fluorescent lights and not a wrinkle crossed her face. Peace enveloped her being and continued to hang in the air as me and the sisters from the local church sighed at the sight of Mum laid out on the porcelain slab.

In many Pentecostal churches I attended, the senior pastor referred to members of the congregation as sisters or brothers. They supported him in his work to ensure the smooth running of the church. Instead of using Mr or Mrs, it is also a respectful way of identifying members of the congregation who have roles or responsibilities within the church. These roles may include warden, choirmaster, youth leader, Sunday school teacher or outreach worker, etc. Together with the vocational skills they have, this strengthens the role of the church and the wider community.

In other cultures and faiths it is not unusual for the elders to carry out sacraments for someone's passing. My sister Elaine was also a member of the church, and the sisters were known to the family and were there to support me and honour Mum.

Immediately they began singing as they busied themselves washing and dressing her in a beautiful white gown. I watched over her patiently, waiting for when it was my turn to fix her hair. Slowly and in unison, the sisters moved Mum from side to side, holding her with such care and tenderness, showing her great respect for her life. The undertaker stood in the distance, observing everyone just in case we needed assistance, but these women were professionals and carried on the tradition of her laying out with precision.

Once they had finished and she was dressed, I began to brush Mum's silky hair. As I lifted her head, it fell off the stool with a loud thud. Everyone stopped and gasped as a trickle of blood released from her nose. Immediately the undertaker stepped forward and said, "Sorry, Mrs Douglas," and proceeded to fill her nostril with cotton wool – not a pretty sight. It made me shiver, but it solved the problem and stemmed the bleed. He gently repositioned her head and nodded at the sisters for me to continue.

Once I was satisfied that all her curls were in place, I applied the final touch: her favourite lipstick. Not too red and not too dark. I smiled at her and squeezed her gloved hand. Tears filled my eyes and trickled down my cheeks as I stood looking at my mum for the last time. I felt the strong arm of one of the church sisters pull me towards her and hug me into her chest as I cried. After a final blessing and one last look, I said goodbye and left her in the charge of the kind undertaker.

Those last few precious moments with my mum and the sisters of the church were an unforgettable time in my life. I was able to make her look beautiful before she went to join her maker and it also helped with the start of my own grieving process. The funeral service and burial were very much a haze, but I take comfort in cherishing the happy memories I continue to share with my friends and family. People said such wonderful things about my mum and I was left in no doubt about how much she was loved.

Agatha Jean Douglas (née Moulton), you were an amazing woman of great dignity. You touched so many of our lives. You were well respected and of great importance. You touched the hearts of everyone you met. May the divine Father watch over you and keep you safe now and forever.

RIEP 31 May 1931–21 November 1986

Epilogue

Special Constabulary

I continued to attend St John Ambulance until I was nineteen. In 1983, I applied for the Special Constabulary and I was accepted. Two years earlier, the 1981 Brixton riots caused much unrest between the black community and the police. It was not a popular time for a black person to be joining an organisation that was viewed as racist.

When I spoke to my dad about a career in the police, he told me he had been a special constable in Jamaica before coming to live in the UK. Knowing this, I was more determined than ever to join the police. Dad always supported me and encouraged me to follow my dream. Mum had been concerned, but understood that I needed to do this.

At the time, Patsy and Keith disapproved. They were of that generation who felt suppressed by the police. Friends that they knew frequently had negative encounters with the police and it was not regarded as a good career choice for a black person. I listened to all their arguments, but for me it was not a difficult decision to make.

How could we see change in a white racist organisation if no one was prepared to join it? You had to be in it to change it!

My friends were shocked, but their opinions did not deter me; in fact, many of them said I was brave. Everyone agreed on one thing: they wanted to see change. I wanted to see change, too, and I was going to be involved in that change.

I remained a special until 1988 when, at the age of twenty-four, I joined the regulars. But that's another story completely...

Acknowledgements

Richard Jordan: My amazing husband, who told me that my book wasn't finished yet! You have been my rock and harshest critic from the beginning of my writing journey. Without your stability, who knows where I would be?

Samantha Carr: If it wasn't for the day we stood in the school car park exchanging childhood stories, laughing hysterically and crying, I would never have written this story.

Lis McDermott: My writing mentor and friend, we gelled during our first encounter. Without your support and encouragement, I would never have grown in confidence to believe in myself and finish writing my story.

Patsy Douglas: My eldest sister, the matriarch of the family, 'Mother and African Queen'. Thank you for always believing in me.

Tanya Douglas: My dear niece, who cried when I gave her my first manuscript and insisted that I publish my work.

Yashima Douglas: My dear niece, who smiled with pride when I shared my story with her. Lots of questions from you forced me to think outside the box. You have inspired me to write and love poetry, which has also stretched and challenged the way I write from the heart.

Sandy Osborne: A fellow author…I can say that now. My friend and partner in crime, who has been with me every step of the way over the last thirty-plus years.

Tony Domaille: A playwright and author who I have known for over thirty years. You saw my outspoken character early in my career and shared my sense of humour. Thanks for your advice and honesty.

Bristol University: Thank you for permission to use stills from 'Adventure Playground 1974'.